Prince Konoe Memoir

The Secret Negotiations Between Japan and the U.S. Before Pearl Harbor

D0220354

Pacific Atrocities Education

Prince Konoe Memoir

The Secret Negotiations Between Japan and the U.S. Before Pearl Harbor

presented with related materials by

PACIFIC ATROCITIES EDUCATION

Introduction and Commentary by
Jenny Chan
and Barbara Halperin

Prince Konoe Memoir

The Secret Negotiations Between Japan and the U.S. Before Pearl Harbor

Introduction and Commentary:
Jenny Chan
Barbara Halperin

This book was made possible with the partnership of Education for Social Justice Foundation.

Paperback ISBN: 978-1-947766-27-3

E-book ISBN: 978-1-947766-25-9

Table of Contents

Introduction

Born on October 12th, 1891, Prince Konoe Fumimaro was the 24th head of one of the most ancient and noble Japanese families, the Fujiwara. Dating back to 646, the House of Fujiwara has been one of five Japanese families "Gosekke," meaning five regent families from which Japanese emperors often were chosen. In the 11th century, they ruled over Japan and, in 1202, they took the name of Konoe.

Although Prince Konoe was born into a noble family, he became an orphan at a young age. His mother passed away when he was eight years old, and his father died when Konoe was fourteen. He was then brought up by his uncle, Prince Tokugawa Iesato. As creditors and debtors frequented his house, his friendships diminished. In college, he began reading "extremist literature from Western Europe" and, influenced by Professor Kawakami, a leading Marxian Japanese economist, Konoe became an ardent student of Karl Marx, Tolstoi, and Kropotkin. It was at Kyoto Imperial University where he met Prince Saionji Kinmochi, who became his political mentor.

In 1917, after graduating from Kyoto Imperial University with a degree in Law and Politics, Konoe was named a member of the House of Peers, the upper House of the Imperial Diet under the Constitution of the

Japanese Empire. There were 145 hereditary members, 106 imperial appointees as well as high taxpayers. A year after entering the House of Peers, he joined the Home Ministry as a non-regular staff member. The Home Ministry managed the internal affairs of the Japanese Empire, including local administration, police, public works, and elections, as well as monitoring people. His involvement in the House of Peers was significant, and he led an active campaign to reform it. As the members of the House were not elected by the people, they were responsible for supporting the government along with the Lower House in smoothly executing policies. Konoe's passion for true democracy was obvious. It could be said that "not a single important national issue has failed to receive his thoughtful consideration or to feel his influence before settlement."

Konoe was tall and gangling with hooded eyes, a long face, and the undershot jaw of the Fujiwaras. He was described as very dark, sad, morose, and indolent. Some described him as an effete aristocrat who was lazy, cynical, confused, and voluptuary with wandering intellectual interests and no strong convictions. He was said to be "a bundle of nerves" and so fussy about hygiene that he sprinkled alcohol on an apple before eating it and dipped raw fish in boiling water before touching it. He also suffered from insomnia. For recreation, he enjoyed watching wrestling matches and playing golf. One report described him as very amiable and was quite interested in literature. Among his friends were the novelists Kikuchi Kan and Yamamoto Yuzo.

However, even in his early days of working in the government, he continued reading Marx and other Western literature and even thought of renouncing his titles, like his brother had, and moving to the United States. It should be noted that his brother, Viscount Konoe Hidemaro, renounced his royal ranking when he chose to become a professional musician. In 1918 before the Paris Peace Conference, Prince Konoe Fumimaro published an essay titled 英米本位の平和主義を排す "Reject the Anglo-American-Centered Peace," setting forth his beliefs on the principles of governing the peace and happiness of mankind. In it, he attacked the western democracies as hypocritically supporting democracy, peace, and self-determination, arguing that these countries actually undermined these ideals through their own version of racially discriminatory imperialism. The essay stressed the importance of greater justice among individuals and equality of rights and opportunities among nations.

It was very obvious that Prince Saionji, who was accused by the Nationalists of Japan as being a globalist, took a liking to Prince Konoe and wanted to groom him to be a statesman. In 1919, Prince Saionji convinced Konoe to attend the Paris Peace Conference as his secretary. The conference turned out to be hugely disappointing. During the conference, he was one of the Japanese diplomats who proposed the Racial Equality Proposal for the League of Nations. It received the support of Japan, France, Serbia, Greece, Italy, Brazil, Czechoslovakia, and China. However, it was overturned by U.S. President Woodrow Wilson.

After returning to Tokyo, Konoe devoted himself to repairing his family fortune with a successful marriage as well as connecting with notable friends. He also founded "The Oriental Free Press," whose focus was the constitution of the Japanese Republic headed by the Emperor. Meanwhile, he was very active in politics and often was credited in large part for Japan's adoption of universal manhood suffrage in 1925.

In 1931, he became Vice President of both the House of Peers and the Privy Council. The Privy Council was an advisory council to the Emperor. Their main functions were to advise on proposed amendments to Japan's Constitution, proposed amendments to the 1889 Imperial Household Law, matters of constitutional interpretation, proposed laws and ordinances, proclamations of martial law or declaration of war, treaties and other international agreements, matters concerning the succession to the throne, declarations of a regency under the Imperial Household Law, and all matters submitted by the emperor generally by the advice of the cabinet. In 1933, Konoe became the President of the House of Peers, a position once held by his father, Konoe Atsumaro.

During this time period, Japan was beginning to occupy Manchuria, forming Manchukuo in China. Following the Manchuria Incident, when Japan began its occupation in China, the amicable Japanese-American relationship became impaired. Konoe was then sent to the United States for a good-will tour where he met with many American leaders, including the President and Colonel House.

On February 26th, 1936, a group of young Imperial Japanese Army officers attempted a *coup d'etat* of the Empire of Japan, also known as the Ni-Ni Roku Jiken. Their goal was to purge the government and military leadership of their factional rivals and ideological opponents. The rebels successfully murdered a couple of leading officials and occupied the center of Tokyo. However, they failed to assassinate Prime Minister Keisuke Okada or secure control of the Imperial Palace.

Following this coup, Konoe was offered the premiership for the first time, but he refused, giving ill-health as the reason. Similar to Emperor Hirohito, Prince Konoe, using ill-health as an excuse whenever he was faced with a difficult situation such as too much military pressure, took to his bed and locked the door. The difficult situations were usually resolved when he returned from his sick leave. It had been asserted that he spent one-half of his political days in bed, and many believed he used his frail health as a political weapon. Some people suggested that the basis of his ill health resulted from the deprivation and exhaustion he suffered in the 1923 earthquake when he contracted pleurisy while searching for friends among the ruins.

On June 2nd, 1937, Emperor Hirohito asked Prince Konoe to head a cabinet to succeed the Government of General Hayashi Senjuro; two days later, the first Konoe cabinet was formed. His political doctrine was described as "not doctrines, but common sense." His intention was to promote the "reconciliation of the rival factions." As he put it, his job was to "heal strife and eliminate friction." This was not an easy task as he had to reconcile the army, reconcile the disgruntled civilian parties, and win the electorate's sympathy.

Konoe became the second youngest Prime Minister in Japan's history and, immediately after his appointment, he created a list of prospective ministers for what was soon tagged "the Telephone Cabinet." It consisted of all parliamentary groups and could be described as the broadest in Japan's entire history. There were critics at the time who thought Konoe was setting up a totalitarian government and that he was using his liberal reputation to keep the nation behind the army's policy.

One month after his new cabinet took office, the "China Incident" happened on July 7th, 1937. Prince Konoe again used ill-health as an excuse. In this case, he had a "cold" just before the China-Incident. Prince Konoe was known to be responsible for the "peace program" in China, which represented the basis of Japan's policy in China. On August 28th, 1937, Konoe stated that "Japan's one course is to beat China to her knees, so that she may no longer have the spirit to fight." On September 12th, he declared, "We shall thoroughly chastise the anti-Japanese elements in China, not only for our own safety but for the welfare of the Far East. Our mission is to deprive the enemy of fighting strength, set an objective lesson for all China, and give new life to wholesome elements in China with whom we hope to join hands in the truest spirit of friendship and cooperation." However, some in Japan doubted his statements. Some said that Konoe was willing to condone an unnecessary war with China to prevent murder and revolt at home, and thus accepted the generals' assurances that the war would be won in six months. In the same year, Italy joined Germany and Japan and signed the Anti-Comintern Pact directed against Communist Internationals, specifically against the Soviet Union.

In the spring of 1938, another disagreement arose regarding whether Japan should push strongly in China or limit the risks, and at this time, Prince Konoe had another "cold." Around the same time, there was a bitter debate about the National Mobilization Bill. The bill had suggested 50 clauses to provide for government controls over civilian organizations, including labor unions, nationalization of strategic industries, price controls and rationing, and nationalized the news media to tighten censorship. It also authorized the government to use unlimited budgets to subsidize war productions and compensate manufacturers for losses caused by wartime mobilization. Ultimately, it put the national economy of the Japanese Empire an on wartime footing after the beginning of the Pacific Asia War. The bill was criticized by the Diet as unconstitutional when it was introduced in January 1938, but then the military put pressure on the bill's importance. Throughout the entire debate, Prince Konoe stayed firmly in bed and only rose from it to make a final successful appeal for the bill.

In October 1938, Prince Konoe became an interim Foreign Minister and Overseas Minister. He explained the foreign policy of his government in vague statements. For example, on November 3rd, 1938, he stated,

"Japan will cooperate with foreign nations so long as they understand the true intention of Japan and adopt policies suitable for the new conditions." In November 1938, the Japan-Germany "Cultural Pact" was signed.

On January 4th, 1939, the Konoe Cabinet resigned. One source reported that Konoe resigned because he was unwilling to sanction the army's demand for limiting industrial profits in the winter of 1938. Former United States Ambassador Joseph C. Grew guessed that Prince Konoe resigned for a different reason. Ambassador Grew stated that the extremist views of the Home Minister, Admiral Suetsugu, who advocated a single national party and drastic measures along totalitarian lines, had made the admiral unacceptable to the Diet. Mr. Grew thought that it was not possible to drop the Home Minister alone; hence Prince Konoe had to resign as well. Another source reported that Konoe warmly supported the movement for the constitution of a new totalitarian party. Apart from the Suetsugu factor, it had been known that Konoe had long wanted to resign. Now that Canton and Hankow had fallen, this could be done without adverse psychological effects. Another reason given by the public toward the China conflict and a change in leadership was required to raise the pitch of popular enthusiasm.

Prince Konoe was succeeded as Prime Minister by Baron Hiranuma, and he became a Minister in Hiranuma without Portfolio. Simultaneously, he occupied the position of President of the Privy Council. On June 14th, 1940, when the Abe Cabinet fell, Konoe was again offered the post of Premier. He refused it, and it was given to Admiral Yonai. On June 25th, 1940, Konoe resigned his position as President of the Privy Council. According to the source, this was done so that he could devote all his time to the formation of a single national party, one of his greatest political ambitions.

On July 22nd, 1940, Konoe formed his second cabinet and immediately issued directives to strengthen national defense, change foreign policy, organize a war economy, and institute educational reform. In August 1940, General Koiso Kuniaki was urging strong measures against the Dutch East Indies, which would have meant immediate war with the United States. Again, Prince Konoe used ill-health as an excuse and did not recover until a decision was already made. On September 27th, 1940, the cabinet concluded the Tripartite Pact with Germany and Italy. According to Ambassador Grew, Konoe was completely against the pact but was overridden by War Minister Tojo Hideki and Foreign Minister Matsuoka. In October 1940, Konoe made a statement during a press interview, "If the United States refuses to understand the real intentions of Japan, Germany, and Italy, and persists in challenging those powers, there will be no other course open to them but to go to war." The following November, the Sino-Japanese Treaty was signed with Wang Ching-Wei.

On October 12th, 1940, Konoe formed the Imperial Rule Assistance Association "to rally the nation behind his government." The idea of forming a single great organization for Japan, to replace its numerous political parties, had been a longstanding ambition of Konoe's. He had turned to Sangyo Kumiai (Cooperatives) for guidance in this matter as early as 1935. Some critics believed that Konoe's original intentions were to meet the military and extremist demands through the creation of the Imperial Rule Assistance Association, eliminating political parties in response to hotheaded cries for "a new political structure," "a new economic structure," "imperial socialism," and more. He sought to channel these demands away from the sort of totalitarianism characterized by a single individual as dictator. Konoe regarded a dictator of the European type as a threat to the Emperor system and as foreign to Japanese traditions of joint responsibility by small groups under the Emperor, and he favored totalitarianism as a general principle. Thus he sought to pilot Japan into a world in which democracy had been liquidated, without sacrificing any of the ancient Japanese traditions while still taking advantage of the opportunities for land grabbing offered by a chaotic world. He had entrusted his friends Count Arima Yoriyasu and Goto Fumio in establishing the new organization.

In an address to the first session of the Preparatory Committee, on August 28th, 1940, Konoe first disclosed his plans. He explained that the new single party he envisaged, was to be "the expression of demand by the will of the nation, transcending cabinet faction or individual." His opinion was that whether or not Japan could firmly establish such a strong national structure, would decide the rise or fall of the nation. An advantage of Konoe at this point was that he had many organizations on which he could lean for support, despite the fact that the

Imperial Rule Assistance Association was not supposed to be political. As stated by its founder, the Imperial Rule Assistance Association was to transmit the "will" of those above. Konoe stated that the constitution guaranteed free speech and association. Therefore, the new organization was not to be an imitation of the Nazi or Fascist party. In Germany and Italy, the party had forced the head of state to make its chief the Premier. To prevent this from happening in Japan, the Premier was to be the head, and he was to appoint directors of the movement, who a new Premier might change. According to the theory, therefore, whoever ran the Imperial Rule Assistance Association would not rival the head of the state. The Premier at the time, Konoe, thus became the Imperial Rule Assistance Association's first President. He chose Count Arima Yoriyasu as the organization's first Director-General and also included such extremists as Admiral Suetsugu Nobumasa, Nakano Seigo, and Hashimoto Kingoro in the directorate. Konoe had pictured the Imperial Rule Assistance Association as a national movement with a "Diet Club" composed of all political factions. Criticism soon was heard on all sides, and when a reorganization was demanded, Konoe quickly retired to bed. When the pressure became heavier, he "recovered" and after consultations with Army and Navy representatives and leaders of the former political parties, he made a number of changes, including eliminating Count Arima and 40 other high Imperial Rule Assistance Association officials. The organization's functions were confined to educational and spiritual affairs, and, according to the press, the organization became far removed from what Konoe had intended.

On April 13th, 1941, the Konoe government signed the Soviet-Japanese Neutrality Pact, making Japan a double-sided Asian power, as Japan had signed treaties with both Germany and Russia. Three weeks after Germany attacked Russia, the cabinet resigned. The Emperor then asked Prince Konoe to form a new government. He decided to drop Foreign Minister Matsuoka, who had concluded the treaties with Germany and Russia and, on July 18th, 1941, two days after the second Konoe cabinet resigned, the third Konoe Cabinet took office. According to Ambassador Grew, both Prince Konoe and the new Foreign Minister Toyoda Teijiro eagerly began efforts for a quick agreement with the United States.

During the summer of 1941, Konoe made several attempts through Ambassador Grew to improve relations with the United States. On August 18th, Foreign Minister Toyoda secretly submitted a proposal to Ambassador Grew, suggesting that Prince Konoe and President Roosevelt meet. Konoe offered to go to Honolulu, an unprecedented step in Japanese history. Mr. Grew wrote that the first suggestion for such a meeting was breached in April. According to Ambassador Grew, Konoe was fully aware of the objections to this move in certain parts of his country. Knowledge, though not content, of the proposal, leaked out and revealed to the pro-Axis and extremist elements in Japan that Prince Konoe had taken the initiative in what was obviously a conciliatory move, at a time when indignation against America was high. Consequently, there were fears of an attempt on Konoe's life. In spite of these risks, the Prince kept pressing Grew for a meeting with President Roosevelt. However, this meeting never took place because the Japanese military began to add stipulations, and President Roosevelt's advisers allegedly became suspicious of the whole proposed meeting.

At the same time, Admiral Nomura, who was Japan's ambassador in Konoe's cabinet, met with Roosevelt to suggest meeting in Juneau, Alaska. On September 3rd, 1941, a liaison conference was held where it was decided that Konoe would continue to seek peace with Roosevelt, but Japan was not going to abandon the Tripartite Pact and would commit to war if a peace agreement did not materialize by mid-October. Konoe and Saionji, as well as their supporters, drafted this proposal, which emphasized the willingness to withdraw troops from China. However, Konoe did not introduce this proposal, the difference in the proposals being that the foreign ministry was conditioned on an agreement being reached between China and Japan before troops could be withdrawn.

Mr. Grew reported that on September 18th, 1941, there was an attack on Premier Konoe's life. Four men armed with daggers and short swords jumped on the running board of his car as he was leaving his private residence. However, the doors were locked, and the assassins were quickly overpowered by the plain-clothes men at the residence.

Konoe met with Tojo privately on October 5 and 7 to convince Tojo to withdraw his troops. In the October 7th meeting, Konoe told Tojo that "military men take wars too lightly." Tojo replied, "Occasionally, one must gather up enough courage, close one's eyes, and jump off the platform of the Kiyomizo." Konoe responded that it was okay for an individual, "but if I think of the national policy that has lasted 2600 years and of the hundred million Japanese belonging to this nation, I, as a person in the position of great responsibility, cannot do such a thing." But in both cases, he failed.

On October 16th, 1941, the cabinet resigned. The following explanation of the resignation was given by Otto D. Tolischus in the Tokyo Record: "The same two irreconcilable schools of thought which had deadlocked the second Konoe Cabinet had carried over into the third. These two schools divided on the issue of whether Japan should reach an agreement with the United States at the cost of substantial concessions or should pursue her immutable national policies by lining up with Germany under the Axis alliance. The final domestic showdown had now come, and there could be little doubt of the outcome. Prince Konoe was through, and the next government would be a military one. Konoe had staked everything on the success of his 'peace message' to Roosevelt. However, slow progress of the Washington negotiations, coupled with the precautionary defense arrangement of the ABCD Powers, which Japan chose to regard as encirclement, the new Germany victories in Russia, and the threatened depletion of Japan's defense resources, had pulled the ground out from under his feet, and the gangs closed in on him. The nationalist radicals, the professional patriots, the political adventurers, the

Toyamas and Nakanos, and their gunmen, the whole 'Manchurian Gang,' which had been working for this day since 1931, could not plead concern over the national fortunes as an excuse for their drive to power. In fact, the cabinet split wide apart and quit. It was perhaps the most courageous deed of Konoe's whole career that he squarely put responsibility where it belonged and, by proclaiming disagreement publicly, disassociated himself from the 'Manchurian Gang.' He had ridden the tiger as long as he could; now, he suffered the fate of all who had tried that feat. I recalled a smiling comment on Konoe, which his secretary, Ushiba, had once made to me: 'No, Konoe is no Samurai.' He could not fight, and after two hours of trying to talk him into it, the Emperor had to let him go." Ambassador Grew wrote that a reasonable motive for Prince Konoe's resignation was the latter's belief that the conversation with the United States would make more rapid progress if that government were dealing with a Prime Minister whose power was based on a commanding position in and support of the army, which is the controlling force in matters affecting policy, rather than with a go-between.

Konoe's resignation could be described as little short of a national catastrophe. The Japanese People had felt "safe" with him at the helm. In fact, at the time, Konoe had been the only Premier who had been very popular with the masses. In spite of his failure to hold the military in check, Prince Konoe came nearer to being a real executive Prime Minister than any of his recent predecessors. Similar to most Japanese liberals, Konoe belonged to no political party and was disposed to dislike them. His one ruling idea throughout his career seemed to be the necessity to stand between the Emperor and the encroachment of the military, resulting perhaps from the fact that his ancestors had always sided with the Emperor against the military clans. As a mature governmental leader, he had shown a tendency to fall away from laissez-faire and to drift toward state control. His headship of three cabinets in recent years demonstrated a sympathetic attitude toward the military powers, and his removal in the fall of 1941 indicates not so much a fall from their grace as a need for firm military control for the conduct of the war.

Commenting on Konoe's relations with the military, Ambassador Grew wrote about the Prince's difficulties with the Imperial Rule Assistance Association, stating, "Essential to his (Konoe's) plan of eliminating the danger of a new shogunate and curbing reckless expansion abroad was the participation of the militarists in the new totalitarian hierarchy, by whose decisions they would have to abide. The Army and Navy recognized Konoe's intention to bind their hands by involving them in a new dictatorship with businessmen and aristocrats and declined the invitation to join. They explained that by agreeing to 'support' the new structure, they meant support from the 'outside,' not the 'inside.' The difference was between controlling Konoe and being controlled by him. The militarists preferred the former and, therefore, remained officially on the 'outside.' Instead of tricking the militarists into assuming responsibility, Konoe was tricked by them into becoming Premier for a second time and committing himself to a program of liquidating all opposition to their foreign policy of aggression and regimenting the nation for total war. He was the most suitable man for the job, as he already had proved himself capable of ramming dictatorial wartime legislation through an unwilling Diet during his first administration. What the militarists wanted Konoe to do during his second administration, when they already had decided to conquer 'Greater East Asia,' was to invoke with a minimum of friction the provisions of his legislation, which was called the National General Mobilization Law. Once set in motion, Konoe was like a ball that continued rolling under its own momentum against gravity. He did not have enough courage to resign in September 1940, when the militarists went back on their pledge made to him in July. Having placed the Emperor, the aristocracy, and the business groups in greater peril than ever, Konoe could not let them down and was obliged to control as best he could the dangerous machine he had organized..."

Following the fall of the third Konoe cabinet, Ambassador Joseph Grew summed up the Prince's position as follows, "... the distinguished service which he had rendered his country. Some people might quibble at that statement, on the grounds that he had led his country into all sorts of difficulties, including the Axis Alliance. I grant all that, but I put it down more to the nefarious influence of Matsuoka than to Konoe himself, who had his own military people, extremists, to deal with. The chief reason why I mentioned his outstanding service was the fact that he alone tried to reverse the engine, and tried hard and courageously, even risking his life and having a very close call as it was. Whatever mistakes he made in directing Japan's policy, he had the sense and the courage to recognize those mistakes and to try to start his country on a new orientation of friendship with the United States..."

Shortly after the formation of the second Konoe Cabinet, Ambassador Grew described Konoe as "a man of the weak physique, poor health, and weak will, who was most reluctantly catapulted into his present position, owing to his family name and tradition and by the force of irresistible circumstance." In November 1940, Grew considered Konoe as "hardly more than a figurehead." In August 1941, he wrote, "In Tokyo, although many of the younger officials in the Government are now strongly anti-American, a stabilizing influence is exerted by Prince Konoe in whom lies the only hope for adjusting American-Japanese relations." Otto Tolischus, in the Tokyo Record, described Konoe in March 1941 as "the best hope there was." He commented that Konoe was pushed forward by the Emperor to stem the totalitarian tide, which threatened to engulf them all. The Prince's prestige made him acceptable to the nation, and the absence of personal ambition or strong convictions made him acceptable to the dominant group. There were reports on how Konoe also frequently called on Toyama Mitsuru, the head of the Kokuryukai (Black Dragon Society) for advice. It should be noted that Konoe had always been a compromiser and had no strong convictions of his own. Conveniently, he often used "illnesses" as an excuse when the political situation became rough.

Not until the Japanese surrender did Konoe again enter the cabinet. Yet he remained a prominent figure in Japanese public life as an active member of the Council of Senior Statesmen. On August 30th, 1943, according to Berlin Radio, Konoe and various other senior statesmen invited the cabinet members to a conference on matters of foreign and domestic policy. On October 29th, 1943, according to Radio Tokyo, he was to be presented at a dinner hosted by Kokuryukai (Black Dragon Society). The same source reported on January 15th and again on May 18th, 1944, that he had attended meetings with Premier Tojo. The same year, on July 18th, he participated in a special meeting called for the purpose of determining who should lead the government after the resignation of the Tojo cabinet. Again during the cabinet of General Koiso, Kuniako was his close personal friend. Konoe attended conferences at the Premier's residence on October 11th and on December 13th, 1944. A Tokyo broadcast declared on October 13th, 1944, that Konoe declined Koiso's offer of the Presidency of the House of Peers, and that Prince Tokugawa Kuniyuki was appointed instead. One source interpreted this as an attempt on the part of Koiso to shelve Konoe. The source continued that there were, at that time, suggestions that a drastic reform of the House of Peers was necessary, which may have been designed to persuade Konoe that this was a big enough job for him. However, the Prince showed no interest. He also made it known that a "fever" prevented him from visiting Wang-Ching-Wei in June.

On November 3rd, 1944, Konoe, along with German ambassador Stahmer, took part in the celebration of the tenth anniversary of the German Institute for Cultural Investigations in Kyoto. On December 26th, 1944, Konoe was elected Honorary President of the 1300th-anniversary celebration of the "Reformation of the Taika Era," to be held in Otsu, Shiga-ken, at the Grand Shrine. On April 5th, 1945, he attended a meeting at the residence of Premier Suzuki. The previous March 28th, Tokyo Radio had reported that he had been mentioned as the possible head of a new party, but had declined, like Kobayashi Seizo. A February 22nd, 1945 report from the United States Intelligence Department stated that Tani Masayuki said that Konoe was asked to form a new cabinet, but that he had suggested Prince Higashi-Kuni Naruhiko. The same source reported that Konoe organized the Otsuorisha Society and was determined to discuss peace. Two other reports mentioned Konoe's name in connection with possible peace moves at the time. A July 10th, 1945 report stated that, upon instructions "from above," several men would be ready to start peace feelers immediately, irrespective of the military's attitude. Among those mentioned was Prince Konoe. A September 14th, 1945 article in the New York Times stated: "last June several peace plotters were arrested by the gendarmerie." Involved were five prominent Japanese, including two described as friends of the former United States Ambassador Joseph Grew. They supposedly had addressed resolutions to Prince Konoe, which were brought to the attention of the police. May 26th, 1945, Paris report asserted that the Japanese government, at the time, planned to send him to Moscow to obtain assurance that Russia would stay neutral in the Far Eastern war. In exchange, Konoe was to offer Russia a free hand in the Manchurian economic field. A Finnish diplomat returning from Japan stated, on May 11th, 1945, that Prince Konoe lived at Karuizawa as did all the neutral diplomats. A source asserted that the Prince refused to receive him because of his fear of the police.

On August 17th, 1945, Konoe was named Vice Premier and Minister without Portfolio in the cabinet of Prince Higashi-Kuni Naruhiko. On September 14th, Konoe visited General MacArthur's headquarters at Yokohama for an unannounced purpose. In an interview with American correspondents on September 13th, 1945, Konoe asserted that he had received the surrender news with "mixed emotions." He said that he had tried to avert war with China and that the militarists started the Peking Incident without government knowledge. He also said that he could have averted war with America if the militarists had let him. He added that neither he nor the Japanese people knew of the Pearl Harbor plans. In an earlier interview, Konoe had asserted that the military was responsible for the breakdown of the proposed meeting with President Roosevelt in the summer of 1941. Konoe added, "The Emperor and I, and most of the cabinet were for acceptance of the American terms that we withdraw from China, but Tojo, with the backing of the military, violently opposed, I had no choice but to withdraw." On September 13th, he also stated that he had taken General Tojo Hideki into his government in 1940 because he had been power-less to oppose Field Marshal Hata Shunroku, who had picked Tojo. He blamed the clash of authority between the military and civil government as the basis for the Japanese government's international reputation as a lie. Konoye also explained that he founded the Imperial Rule Assistance Association in 1940 to give the civil government an instrument to control the military "through the united support of the people" and not to impose a Nazi or Fascist government on the nation. However, he added, it did not work. In the end, the militarists took hold of the idea and used it for their own purposes. In an interview on September 14th, 1945, Konoe declared that during the past three years, he had been followed, dogged, and threatened by the Kempeitai, the secret military police. In the same interview, he asserted that he and Generalissimo Chiang Kai-shek probably could have reached an agreement. However, when he was dispatched as personal emissary to the Chinese leader, the Japanese military physically grabbed him as he boarded a ship at Kobe.

An article in the Washington Post of September 9th, 1945, stated that Japanese intellectuals, who opposed the warlords' schemes, are preparing their own list of war criminals. Two close supporters of Prince Higashi-Kuni said that Prince Konoe should be on the list, too. However, after the surrender, General MacArthur wanted Prince Konoe to come forward and lead a revision of the constitution and other reform, as well as starting a new political party. Konoe agreed to form a committee to revise the constitution. After the Americans occupied Japan, Konoe refused to collaborate with U.S. Army officer Bonner Fellers in "Operation Blacklist" to exonerate Hirohito and the imperial family of criminal responsibility. In December 1945, Konoe consumed potassium cyanide and committed suicide. A week before he committed suicide, he wrote this memoir.

Prince Konoe in the fall of 1941 before the attack on Pearl Harbor

Propaganda on the Axis of Power in 1938.
Hitler (left) Konoe (middle) Mussolini (right)

1936 Prince Konoe as the President of the House of Peers

Prince Konoe in his 20s

Memoir by Prince Konoe

Preface

During the Konoye Cabinet, American-Japanese negotiations took place from April to October 1941. Initially,
the talks were conducted in complete secrecy but, as
leaks occurred, various inferences based on inadequate
evidence became known, leading to criticism and attacks
on the government. I held onto hope until the last minute, since reasons existed supporting the avoidance of
an American-Japanese conflict. First was the outbreak of
the Reich-Soviet War. The second was the naval leaders'
views. The third reason involved the matter of materials.

The Tripartite Alliance was concluded based on the
premise of a linked German-Soviet-Japanese relationship
but was invalidated when the Reich-Soviet War broke
out. The Soviet Union ran to the Anglo-American camps
leaving Japan in the worst situation, i.e., we might be
compelled to regard the United States and the Soviet
Union as enemies. Regarding this, I refer you to a separate article on the Tripartite Alliance.

Admiral Oikawa Approves Alliance

Regarding the conclusion of the Tripartite Treaty, I
thought the Navy initially would not approve the pact.

This assumption was based on the Navy's attitude during the days of the Hiranuma Cabinet.

At the time of the Cabinet organization, Navy Minister Zengo Yoshida agreed to the idea of strengthening the Tripartite Axis. As the talks developed, however, the Tripartite Alliance proposed stipulations on military aid which became significantly worrisome for the Navy and Minister Yoshida. Eventually, a worsening heart condition forced him to resign.

When Admiral Oikawa became the Navy Minister, the Navy abruptly approved the Tripartite Alliance, arousing my suspicion. The then Vice-Minister Toyoda, commenting on the circumstances, said:

"Truthfully, at heart, the Navy is opposed to the Tripartite Pact, but since the domestic political situation no longer permits further opposition on the Navy's part, the Navy unavoidably approves it, albeit, for political reasons. From a military standpoint, the Navy has no confidence in fighting the United States."

I said "This is something I did not expect. Politics is something which no statesman deals with and the Navy need not be concerned with it. The Navy should examine the matter purely from a military standpoint and, if it lacks confidence, it should oppose it to the end. Isn't that the way to demonstrate loyalty to the country?"

Vice-Minister Toyoda said "Now that the situation has come to this point, please try to understand the Navy's position. Other than diplomatic negotiations, there is no longer any other way to prevent the increased obligation of military assistance in the Tripartite Pact."

Shortly afterward, I saw Admiral Isoroku Yamamoto, Commander-in-Chief of the Combined Fleet, when he came up to Tokyo. The Admiral was strongly opposed to the Tripartite Alliance. The obstinate opposition of the then Navy Minister Yonai to the Tripartite Alliance in the Hiranuma Cabinet days seemed to have been strong due to then Vice-Minister of the Navy Yamamoto's assistance.

When I shared with Admiral Yamamoto what Vice-Minister Toyoda told me, the Admiral said "If I am told to fight regardless of the consequences, I shall run wild considerably for the first six months or year, but I have utterly no confidence for the two years. The Tripartite Pact has been concluded as is. In light of the situation, I hope you will endeavor to avoid an American-Japanese war."

Thus, if the Navy's mind was clearly ascertained, I thought the actual application of the Tripartite Pact needed to be done both with considerable care and circumspection. Even if the Soviet Union were to side with the Allies, given the Navy's view, an American-Japanese conflict had to be avoided to the extent permitted by circumstances.

Naval Leaders Still Cautious

When American-Japanese negotiations began, both the Army and Navy enthusiastically hoped for a successful conclusion. By August, however, the Army's enthusiasm had begun to diminish. I heard strong views from lower-ranked naval officers and when questioned, they responded unconcernedly "We shall control such blind movements."

At a liaison conference, the Chief of the Naval General Staff declared clearly "If the United States alone is the other party, we have some confidence in fighting, but if the Soviet Union enters the conflict, requiring us to conduct operations in the north and the south, our confidence will be gone."

When October arrived and my cabinet members were on the verge of resigning, naval leaders still favored continuing American-Japanese negotiations. In view of their relations with the Army and the internal relations of the Navy, they did not openly state their preference. Instead, they entrusted the matter to the Prime Minister.

The third reason to avoid a Japanese-American conflict concerned our dependence on the United States and Britain for munitions, which made us vulnerable. Several times I ordered the Planning Board to look for alternatives to possibly eliminate this vulnerability but, invariably, the result was "impossible."

The normalization of American-Japanese trade and economic activities in the Southwest Pacific constituted one area of American-Japanese negotiations aimed at acquiring the needed munitions.

In the course of the negotiations, however, the United States invoked the Asset-Freezing Act which blocked the acquisition and replenishment of materials. Since the continual decrease of goods in storage would lead to what was called "jirihin" (general impoverishment), the problem became acute.

Tojo Asserts Severance of Economic Relations Means Gradual Impoverishment

Feared gradual impoverishment was the fundamental reason for the insistence of war advocates that war with the United States should commence as soon as possible. Two ways were considered to prevent the exhaustion of war materials. The first was to obtain materials freely by a successful conclusion of American-Japanese negotiations. The second was to meet military demands by promoting domestic production capacity. This is seen as one of the major reasons for the government's concerted efforts to successfully conclude U.S.-Japan negotiations.

Replenishment of Munitions and Petroleum

At a critical stage of American-Japanese negotiations, the government again ordered the Planning Board to conduct investigations into war materials, resulting in the following report.

"The most difficult problem at hand is petroleum since other materials possibly may be obtained. 500,000 tons of petroleum might be acquired towards the end of 1943 and 4,000,00 tons in the course of 1944, provided the petroleum industry is extended with the capital of Y2,000,000,000.

Even if the Dutch East Indies is captured by force, the enemy will destroy its oil facilities without fail. Moreover, the matter of transportation must be considered. Therefore, in the first year, we cannot expect to have more than 300,000 tons of oil and more than 1,500,000 tons in the second year. It may take five or six years before 5,000,000 can be obtained."

The foregoing report made known the impossibility of obtaining our required amount of petroleum even by the use of armed force and that the goal of preventing the gradual exhaustion of war materials would be attained by extending the artificial petroleum industry.

On September 6, 1941, a decision made at the Imperial Conference stated: "There shall immediately be made a determination to declare war on the United States (Britain and Holland)" in the event that, as late as early October, our demands in the American-Japanese negotiations have not been met." However, thinking a successful conclusion to the negotiations was a possibility, there was no objection to the hesitation of the war declaration. Even if the negotiations were unsuccessful, the Imperial Conference declaration did not say "We should open war." It merely said that we should determine to open war. Therefore, the means of going to war remained with only economic relations severed. In fact, the government considered the second course in case of what they considered inevitable.

It is Domestic Politics that Starts War

On the other hand, war advocates stubbornly persisted on the grounds that war materials gradually would be exhausted. I said to Planning Board President Suzuki, "If fostering domestic production capacity could prevent the exhaustion of petroleum and other war materials, support should be extended even at the cost of many billions. Isn't it very stupid to obtain these materials at the great cost of war with the United States and Britain?" Suzuki replied, "Yes, it is as you say, but it is domestic politics that starts the war."

In due course, the Cabinet resigned en bloc and the situation seemed helpless. Later, at a conference of senior statesmen on November 29, 1941, shortly before the Tojo Cabinet plunged Japan into war, I questioned Premier Tojo.

"Isn't it possible to prevent gradual exhaustion of war materials through domestic production? And, if possible, Japan needs not absolutely initiate war against the United States, Britain, and Holland. What do you think of the policy of not resorting to war while only economic relations are ruptured, thereby providing a means to resolve the situation?"

Premier Tojo replied, "Since the inception of the Cabinet, our efforts were focused on this issue. However, since we have concluded that we shall sink into a state of gradual impoverishment if we continue without recourse to war with only economic relations cut off, we have at last decided to open war." Premier Tojo said gradual impoverishment was unavoidable but Planning Board President Suzuki agreed that this was preventable. Therefore, one of the two was lying. President Suzuki's remark, "It is domestic politics that starts the war," seemed very significant.

As previously stated, I endured criticism and other trials for about six months and persistently continued American-Japanese negotiations for the previously mentioned three reasons. Below is a brief description of the progress and circumstances of the negotiations.

Pros and Cons on the 7-Point American Proposal

Since around December 1940, talks began among Bishop Walsh of the widely known Catholic school, Maryknoll, Mr. Draft, Chief Secretary of Maryknoll, Postmaster General Walker and Colonel Iwahata of the Military Affairs Bureau War Office and Mr. Tadao Ikawa regarding the adjustment of American-Japanese relations. In April 1941, Japan and the United States were open to discussing the matter. Notably, the American president and Secretary of State Hull on the American side and Ambassador Nomura and the military and naval attaches of the Japanese Embassy in Washington on the Japanese side confidentially established contact and had full knowledge of the talks going on between civilians of both countries.

On April 8, the Americans put forward the first test plan. The Japanese revised it and put forward a second test plan. On April 14 and 16, Secretary of State Hull invited Ambassador Nomura to hold initial talks with him. Mr. Hull then declared that the civilian talks could be shifted to unofficial continued talks between himself and Ambassador Nomura.

Between the afternoon of April 17 and the morning of April 18, Ambassador Nomura's cable containing the important offer reached the Foreign Office here. At that time, Foreign Minister Matsuoka was in Siberia on the way back from Europe. At 11:00 AM on April 18, Vice-Minister Chuichi Ohashi of the Foreign Office gave me the first report during the Cabinet Council meeting. At 4:30 PM, the Vice-Minister called on me, accompanied by Director Terazaki of the American Bureau. The following is the full text of the plan.

Points of American-Japanese Understanding:

- The Japanese and United States governments hereby accept responsibility for the purpose of negotiating and concluding a general agreement aimed at restoring relations and traditional friendship between the two countries.
- The two governments sincerely hope to prevent a repetition of the incidents which have aggravated the friendly feelings between the people of both countries, to be conscious of unexpected events,

and to discuss particularly the causes of the recent estrangement of relations.

- Both governments acutely hope that peace will be established in the Pacific by joint endeavors on the basis of morality, that the menace of deplorable disturbances calculated to destroy culture will be dispelled by early completion of close and friendly understanding between the United States and Japan, and should that be found impossible, a further extension will be prevented.

American-Japanese relations will be substantially adjusted if the following points are clarified or improved:

1. The international and state idea entertained by Japan and the United States
2. The attitude of both governments toward the European war
3. Relations between both governments regarding the China Affair
4. Relations of the naval strength, air strength, and shipping in the Pacific
5. Trade and financial collaboration between both countries
6. The economic activity of both countries in the Southwest Pacific area
7. The policy of the two governments concerning the political stabilization of the Pacific

By the foregoing considerations, the following understanding has been reached and will be subject to the

Japanese government's final and formal decision after undergoing revisions by the American government.

The international idea and state idea as entertained by Japan and the United States:

- The Japanese and American governments mutually recognize that they are equal and independent countries and neighboring Pacific powers. They propose to clarify their unity and desire for lasting peace and for bringing about a new era of trust and cooperation based on mutual respect.
- Both governments state their traditional confidence in the rights of various countries and races, the adjustment of mutual interests, and the maintenance of the protected, peaceful pursuit of their spiritual and material welfare.
- Both governments are strongly determined to maintain their own traditional state ideas, social order and moral principles which are the basis of their national life and not permit opposing foreign ideas to run unrestrained.

The attitude of the two governments regarding the European war:

The Japanese government hereby clarifies that the purpose of the Axis Alliance is defensive and endeavors to prevent the extension of the relations of military linking to non-participating states in the European war. It is hereby declared that the military obligation based on the Axis Alliance shall be invoked only when Germany is positively attacked by a state or states now not taking part in the European war.

1. The relations of the two governments concerning the China Affair:

The American president recognizes the following conditions and, moreover, if the Japanese government guarantees them, the American president shall advise peace to the Chiang regime on the basis of:

a) China's independence
b) Withdrawal of Japanese troops from Chinese territory based on a mutual agreement to be entered into by Japan and China
c) Non-annexation of China
d) Non-reparations
e) Restoration of the Open Door Policy
f) The amalgamation of the Chinese regime and the Wang government
g) Self-restraint of large scale or collective emigration of Japanese to Chinese territory
h) Recognition of Manchukuo

If the Chiang regime responds to the American President's advice, the Japanese government shall immediately open peace negotiations directly with the Chinese government to consider being newly unified or the elements to compose the Chinese government.

The Japanese government will submit directly to the Chinese side concrete peace terms within the scope of the foregoing conditions and on the basis of good neighbor friendship, principles of economic cooperation and joint defense against communism.

2. Naval and air strength and shipping relations in the Pacific:

   a) Desiring peace in the Pacific, Japan, and the United States shall not demonstrate any disposition toward the other of naval or air force menace. Therefore, the talks between the two shall consist of concrete details.

   b) Upon concluding the agreement, the two countries shall mutually dispatch their fleets for courtesy calls as a sign of the arrival of peace in the Pacific.

   c) If the China Affair is resolved, the Japanese government, in response to the American government's desire, shall consent to place, chiefly in the Pacific, vessels of its own that may be liberated from service. Its tonnage and other details shall be determined during American-Japanese talks.

3. Trade and financial cooperation between the two countries:

   If the two governments conclude and recognize the agreement, if one party has goods and materials needed by the other, protected acquisition should be assured. Proper means shall be taken for the resumption of legitimate trade relations previously existing during the operation of the American-Japanese Commercial Treaty. Moreover, if a new commercial treaty is desired, the matter shall be studied in American-Japanese negotiations and concluded in accordance with usual customs. To expedite economic cooperation, the United States shall offer Japan gold credits sufficient for realizing commercial and industrial development and economic cooperation aimed at improving economic conditions in East Asia.

4. Economic activities of the two countries in the Southwest Pacific area:

   In view of the peaceful development of Japan in the southwest Pacific, Japan shall receive American cooperation and support regarding production and acquisition of oil, rubber, tin, nickel, and others in areas desired by Japan.

5. The policy of the two countries regarding the stabilization of the Pacific:

   a) In the future, Japan and the U.S. shall not recognize cession or annexation of East Asian territories or the Southwest Pacific by European countries

b) The two countries shall jointly guarantee Philippine independence and consider providing assistance in the event of an unprovoked attack by a third country

6. Japanese emigration to the United States and Southwest Pacific shall be given friendly consideration and equal treatment as with other countries

American-Japanese Negotiations

a) Honolulu will be the site of talks by representatives of the two countries. President Roosevelt and Prime Minister Konoye will represent the United States and Japan, respectively. Each side will have no more than five representatives, excluding experts and secretaries.

b) No third country observers will be permitted to participate.

c) The talks will begin as soon as the current understanding of materializes (May).

d) Matters previously included in the current understanding shall not be re-discussed.

e) Discussion regarding the previous arrangement will take place between the two governments and written documentation of the understanding created. A concrete agenda shall be agreed upon. Supplementary Rules include writing a confidential memorandum of the items of understanding and both governments shall agree on the scope, nature and period of the announcement.

Liaison Conference Immediately Held

In view of the issue's importance, I called for a conference between the government and the Supreme Command. The government was represented by the Prime Minister, Home, War, and Navy Ministers, and Vice-Minister of Foreign Affairs while the Supreme Command was represented by the Chiefs of the General Staff and the Naval General Staff. The Military Affairs Bureau, Naval Affairs Bureau Chief, and Chief of Secretary of the Cabinet also were present. The American proposal generated the following views:

1. Acceptance of the American plan would be the greatest shortcut to disposing of the China Affair. The establishment of the Wang government failed to achieve anything and direct negotiations with Chungking had become exceedingly difficult. Since Chungking was now entirely dependent on the United States, direct negotiations with Chungking would not accomplish anything unless the United States was designated as an intermediary. In view of that, the foregoing point is clear.

2. Responding to this proposal and seeking rapprochement of Japan and the United States would offer an excellent opportunity to avoid an American-Japanese war. Moreover, it would prevent the

European war from becoming a world war and, instead, could be a prelude to creating world peace.

3. As of now, Japan's national power has been considerably consumed. The China Affair must be solved as soon as possible and efforts made to restore and build national power. The idea of a Southward advance, insisted upon in some sections, is impracticable. Even the Supreme Command has no confidence in it. Even from the standpoint of building national power, it now is necessary for Japan to shake hands with the United States and seek to promote the replenishment of materials for the future.

The majority of those present were in favor of acceptance with the expressed following conditions:

1. Clarification must be made that the American-Japanese agreement does not violate the Tripartite Alliance.

2. Further clarification should be made of the aim of contributing toward world peace through American-Japanese collaboration. If the agreement leads to American hands-off in the Pacific and strong aid to Britain, it will constitute a lack of faith in Japan's part toward Germany. Accordingly, the American-Japanese collaboration should be well developed and able to offer mediation between Britain and Germany.

3. The content of the present proposal is too complex.

4. The original wording gives one a sense of the old order. There should be greater clarification of the positive side of a newly constructed order.

5. Unless things are done quickly, leaked information will be feared. Accordingly, the Foreign Minister's return to Tokyo should be urged.

Whether or not this matter should be communicated to Germany, the following two views were expressed.

- Such an important issue cannot be communicated to Germany from the standpoint of faith. At least, prior to sending a reply to the United States, Germany should be notified.
- If Germany is notified beforehand, objections may be raised. Accordingly, what could materialize may not. It is better, therefore, to support the talks without notifying Germany.

American Plan Secretly Communicated to Germany

The following is a summary of a history of the American-Japanese negotiations written by the last Prince Konoye in the spring of 1942 after the outbreak of the war. The earlier article captioned "The Circumstances Attending the American-Japanese Negotiations in the

2nd and 3rd Konoye Cabinets" forms a supplement to the following articles. Ed., Asahi.

Matsuoka Proposes Revised Plan

Irrespective of his outward speech and action, it was undeniable that Foreign Minister Matsuoka was secretly concerned about the treatment of American-Japanese issues. Even on his sickbed, he carefully examined the revised plan prepared by the Army, Navy and Foreign Office as well as the original American plan and largely revised it. Thus, on May 3, arrangements were made for the convocation of the third liaison conference. The conference mainly approved the revised plan as prepared by the Foreign Minister. The following were the revision's main points.

The fourth clause of the matters of understanding. "... the relations of the naval and air forces and shipping in the Pacific..." were erased. A new article should be inserted in the clause regarding peace mediation between Britain and Germany at the hands of Japan and the United States, "The Attitude of the Two Governments Regarding the European War." Japan's assurance that it would never make a southward advance by force should be eliminated and the American-Japanese talks should be eliminated.

Matsuoka Proposes Neutrality Pact

While the majority wanted the revised plan communicated to the American side at once, Foreign Minister Matsuoka disagreed and insisted that, first, a new proposal to conclude of a neutrality pact should be made to the United States. The majority ultimately acquiesced.

The next issue was whether or not the present issue should be communicated to Germany. The Foreign Minister was successful in strongly insisting that his diplomatic ability should be trusted. Following the liaison conference, he sent two instructions to Ambassador Nomura. The first was an interim reply to the United States in the form of an oral statement addressed to Secretary of State Hull stating that the Italian and German leaders were confident of their victory and arguing that American participation in the European war would merely prolong it and bring about destruction. It stressed, moreover, that Japan could not impose even the slightest injury on her German and Italian allies.

The second instruction requested Ambassador Nomura to propose, as his impromptu idea, the conclusion of a simple and clear American-Japanese neutrality pact. The following day, May 4, the Foreign Minister went to Western Japan to worship at the Grand Shrine of Ise to report to the spirits of the Imperial Ancestors his return to Japan. During his absence from Tokyo, he sent Director Sakamoto of the Foreign Office European-Asiatic Affairs Bureau to the German and Italian Ambassadors in Tokyo with an interim report stating that the United

States made a proposal for the adjustment of American-Japanese relations, adding that this was a matter of absolute secrecy.

Returning to Tokyo on May 6, Foreign Minister Matsuoka received a visit from the German Ambassador, during which he requested to know Foreign Minister Ribbentrop's views of the proposal. Specifically, Matsuoka said to the German Ambassador "To make a counter-use of the evil intention of the United States and solve the Sino-Japanese Affair would also be an advantage to Germany after all."

The U.S. Turns Down Neutrality Pact

In Washington, while Ambassador Nomura and his staff were very concerned about the long delay of the Japanese reply, interim instructions from Foreign Minister Matsuoka reached the Embassy. On May 7, the Ambassador met Secretary of State Hull and probed the possibility of a neutral pact, which Hull refused to consider. Later, Nomura conducted a confidential investigation into the views of American government leaders, ascertaining that the neutrality pact might not be a bad idea after the plan under discussion materialized, but was unthinkable at the current stage.

Fearing Secretary Hull's feelings might be offended, Nomura failed to hand over a copy of the oral statement and refrained from reading it in its entirety. During the talk, Hull is said to have urged, in an unusually strong tone, opening the negotiations themselves as early as possible.

Thus, Foreign Minister Matsuoka's test plan failed. Quickly, the situation in the United States became more difficult, chiefly through enforcement of the national defense law and the merchantmen convoying issue. Ambassador Nomura repeatedly demanded a reply. The Japanese military and naval office's attaches in Washington communicated to their home country an atmosphere of considerably unreserved opposition to Matsuoka, charging him with what may be called gesture diplomacy. The military attaché in Berlin, on the other hand, sent a telegram to the War Minister saying "According to a report from reliable sources, the Government is negotiating with the United States. We are utterly opposed to such talks. If it warrants our action, we are prepared to make a general withdrawal."

This incident may be regarded as a ripple caused by communication between Germany and Italy.

Matsuoka Urges Throne to Support Axis

As the situation became more confused and complex, the activities of the Cabinet Ministers became more energetic. On being received by the Emperor on May 8, Foreign Minister Matsuoka told the Throne: "In case of American participation in the war, Japan's support of the Italo-German side would lead to a total collapse of the adjustment of American-Japanese relations. In any case, if Japan were to be unfaithful to Germany and Italy due to strong efforts regarding issues with the United States, I shall have to resign."

This report was communicated to me by Matsuoka himself on May 9. That night, I secretly called the War and Navy Ministers to my home and conferred with them regarding measures to be taken regarding Matsuoka's attitude. I also made arrangements with them to call another liaison conference concerning the attitude to be taken by our country in case of American war participation and the appropriate method of action if Germany expressed opposition or revision.

Emperor Seriously Concerned

The following day, May 10, the Emperor received me in the audience. With a very seriously concerned look, he told me the contents of the Foreign Minister's report to the Throne. His Majesty stated: "In case the United States goes to war, Japan will have to attack Singapore. And if the United States comes in, the war will be a protracted affair. As a result, there may be a danger of a Reich-Soviet conflict. In that case, Japan will have to abandon the Neutrality Pact and, taking Germany's side, must go as far as Irkutsk. Such was Matsuoka's statement."

I told His Majesty that the Foreign Minister's report represented nothing but a mere idea to provide in the event of a worst-case scenario. Even if it was Matsuoka's idea, the High Command and the Cabinet Council must approve it before a decision is made. I then implored His Majesty not to worry.

I took the opportunity to tell His Majesty the following. For the purpose of disposing of the China Affair, currently, there is no immediate recourse except to utilize the United States. The present American proposal offers an ideal opportunity and we want to urge it. However, I reported on conflicting views likely to arise within the Cabinet if Germany raised objections to the American-Japanese understanding, America's second revision of the already revised plan, and American war participation after the formation of the American-Japanese understanding. In addition to possible Cabinet members' conflicting views, I detailed a possible split in public opinion. I further stated that I shall encourage things as smoothly as possible but, if not workable, I may need to resort to emergency measures. Hence, I expressed my determination.

His Highness gave his assent to all of my remarks and told me to proceed along that line. I then spoke with Lord Keeper of the Privy Seal, Kido, who revealed that Matsuoka had become too positive in his views since returning from Europe and had lost His Majesty's confidence. Following Matsuoka's departure from the Palace, His Majesty sought Kido's advice on the matter of replacing the Foreign Minister.

American Suspicion Aroused by Our Revised Plan

Germany's reply failed to come. Meanwhile, submission to the United States of the revised plan as decided on May 3 was postponed in spite of repeated requests from the Army and Navy. At last, in view of needing to forward the plan to the Americans prior to the American President's scheduled speech on May 14, on May 12 at noon, the Foreign Minister issued instructions to Ambassador Nomura permitting him to open negotiations though no reply had come from the German side.

Acting on those instructions, on May 11 (May 12 Japanese time), Ambassador Nomura called on Secretary of State Hull and submitted the Japanese revised plan. On May 13, Foreign Minister Matsuoka sent another message to Hull, emphasizing two points as the premise.

1. The United States does not take part in the European War.
2. The United States advises Chiang Kai-shek to open negotiations with Japan for peace.

Secretary of State Hull urged Ambassador Nomura in his response. "The American-Japanese talks now in progress are not negotiations being carried on a certain basis as yet but are informal and free talks. So let us talk unreservedly from the bottom of our heart."

Concerning the revised plan handed to Hull by Nomura, Hull showed more than a little suspicion concerning the omission of the clause pertaining to the guarantee that Japan would not make an armed advance into the Southern regions. Regarding the China Affair items, he was especially concerned and asked many questions. He also made a noteworthy remark that the Secretary must contact Britain regarding the China Affair issue.

Hull, maintaining a considerably cautious attitude, also explained that domestic circumstances in the United States were not of a nature that would render American-Japanese talks easy. The President's May 14 speech was postponed to May 29. The convoy issue was seriously controversial and there were indications that the United States, influenced by domestic and foreign situations, found it difficult to make a decision. In any case, contrary to Japanese expectations, a reply from the United States would not come.

Germany Protests Against Negotiations

Wanting the German reply beforehand, Foreign Minister Matsuoka repeatedly delayed our reply to the United States. Though he tried in vain, he was forced to send instructions to Ambassador Nomura on May 12 asking him to reply to the American side. Shortly after the reply was sent to the United States, Germany replied to Japan saying that the real intention of the United States in seeking a compromise with Japan is to push the matter of participation in the European War. The German side requested the Japanese Government to clarify the fact that the protection and convoying which the United States is carrying on is recognized as an action purposely inciting war in which Japan will be bound to take part. It also clarified the fact that, if the United States refrains from such action, Japan will be prepared to study and weigh the American proposal.

Germany's reply concluded, as well, that in view of the effect the present matter would have on the Tripartite Pact, the final reply should be shown to the German side before it was sent to the United States. The Italian government sent a representative to the Japanese government asking Japan to accept the German reply as Italy's reply as well.

On May 19, Ambassador Ott, as expected, expressed his home government's dissatisfaction with the Japanese government's reply to the Americans before receiving the German reply. He said that a treaty concluded by one of the Tripartite powers with another country weakened the Tripartite Powers Pact, indirectly expressing Germany's basic objections to the American-Japanese negotiations. Ott requested clarification of "the obligation of the United States government not to intervene in the war between Britain and the Axis Powers" and the "obligation of Japan-born of the Tripartite Pact." In conclusion, Ott high-handedly declared:

"The German government must insist on its hope that it will be allowed full participation in American-Japanese negotiations and have immediate information on Japan's reply to the United States. If the Japanese government listens to the U.S. representation without having a previous understanding with the German government on all important issues and defines her position, it will not be fitting in relation to the Tripartite relations."

A telegram from Ambassador Oshima in Berlin also came reporting that the German leaders felt serious antipathy toward American-Japanese negotiations and he expressed strong opposition to the talks.

Matsuoka Holds On

On May 15, a liaison conference was held in Tokyo but nothing concrete was decided beyond the exchange of information and views. The effect of frequent representations from the German government and Ambassador Oshima on Foreign Minister Matsuoka's increasingly vague attitude was noted. While other Cabinet ministers were full of hope, only Matsuoka was opposed. At the May 22 conference, Director Oka of the Naval Affairs Bureau told Chief Secretary of the Cabinet Tomita,

"If the Foreign Minister is opposed to our views, in case an agreement materializes, a split of views within the Cabinet will be feared."

The Foreign Minister spoke with me on May 23, stating "It seems to me that the Army and Navy leaders are endeavoring to have an American-Japanese understanding materialize, even if it impairs our friendship with Germany and Italy, but what can we do with such a weak-kneed attitude?"

Regarding the interpretation of Article Three of the Tripartite Pact, Matsuoka would not cede his strong view that, even if the German side attacked an American convoy, Japan would be obligated to take part in the war and assist Germany, since the convoy itself would be regarded as an attack. This point was repeatedly stressed to American Ambassador Joseph C. Grew. Matsuoka also said that by so doing, United States participation in the war might be prevented.

According to Matsuoka's view, the American President was unwaveringly in favor of war participation. In that case, an American-Japanese understanding would be cast to the wind. In that scenario, the Japanese people would not accept that view and might begin to riot. In any case, Japan would be compelled to clarify her attitude in favor of Britain and the United States or Germany and Italy. He also added his determination to insist on concerted action with Germany and Italy.

In conclusion, Matsuoka said, "As for the idea of His Majesty, I, as a subject of His Majesty, will have to follow it."

His declaration hinted at his resignation as Foreign Minister if warranted under certain circumstances.

Foreign Minister's Attitude Strange

It was suspected that during his stay in Europe, Matsuoka's speech and action hinted that a particular important commitment had been made. As to the content of his talks in Europe, there was no way to believe his reports. According to them, Hitler and Ribbentrop urged Japan to attack Singapore, but he made no commitment. However, a telegram from Ambassador Oshima said: "Foreign Minister Ribbentrop considers Mr. Masuoka to have entirely revised his view regarding an attack on Singapore, a view learned to be his private view during Mr. Matsuoka's visit to Europe."

Seeing this information, the question arises as to which is the truth. At any rate, the real intention of the Foreign Minister then sandwiched between the American issue and the Italo-German obligation was hard to understand. From then, Matsuoka began openly expressing his dissatisfaction and antipathy toward Ambassador Nomura. In the course speaking with me on May 23, he expressed his anger.

"The present proposal was not made by the American side but rather by Ambassador Nomura."

I explained that he had misunderstood, but Matsuoka continued accusing Nomura of having overstepped the limits of his duty. At least when he found that the proposal was not born of his own talk with Steinhardt, Matsuoka began feeling seriously dissatisfied.

According to a report which the Navy picked up sent to the British government from Ambassador Halifax, Nomura told Secretary of State Hull that, while His Majesty and army and navy leaders were hoping for the materialization of American-Japanese talks, Matsuoka alone opposed that. Upon learning this, Matsuoka was quite indignant and cabled instructions to Nomura ordering him to correct the misunderstanding of the Secretary of

State. Nomura replied: "I am utterly surprised at your report. There is absolutely no foundation whatsoever in the rumor." The reply was accompanied by the explanation that Nomura made a statement to the effect that in Japan the foreign policy cannot be determined solely by the Foreign Minister.

To this, Matsuoka sent another telegram. "If the report is baseless, that is alright, but if anyone is found to have given such an impression in your place, proper control must be enacted."

Thus, Matsuoka expressed his antipathy against men close to Nomura, including members of the embassy staff. The issue was settled at the moment but the conflict between Matsuoka and Nomura and his lieutenants resurfaced.

Nomura-Hull Talks Slow

On May 5, 14, 16, 20, 21 and 28, off-the-record discussions continued for from one to three hours amid a friendly atmosphere. The issues concerned an agreement on the Pacific area, the Tripartite Pact, and the China issue but there were no signs of rapid development. Based on the tone of the Secretary of State's talks and confidential investigations, it appeared true that the American government was dubious of Japan having any sincere intention to bring negotiations to a successful conclusion, particularly since the United States had a strongly guarded view of Foreign Minister Matsuoka and others.

The American President delivered a fireside chat open to the attention of the world on May 27 that made no direct reference to Japan and only slightly touched on China. There was a report that special attention was paid to relations with Japan which reflected America's cautious attitude. However, some of the American press said that, prior to the fireside chat, the President invited congressional leaders to a conference where he expressed having a less vigorous policy toward Japan and addressed the matter of fighting Germany. The American President was credited with saying: "In Japan, the opposition of financial circles against the Army's policy has become influential and this is bound to develop to a point where the Tripartite Pact will be virtually nullified." In Tokyo, this piece of news was banned, but the Foreign Minister believed the ban should be lifted immediately. On May 30 he issued a public statement stating that the Axis diplomacy was absolutely immutable and that there is a limit to the policy of a peaceful Southern advance.

Reich-Soviet War Opens

I went to Western Japan on June 13 and returned on June 16. The following day, Wang Ching-wei of the National Government came to Tokyo to stay until June 25, when much of my time was committed. Meanwhile, on June 22 I received an urgent report from Europe on the opening of the Reich-Soviet War.

Strangely, the American reply had been received one day before the astounding news of the Reich-Soviet War was received. Dated June 21, it was given to Ambassador Nomura and cabled to Tokyo on June 24. The Cabinet found it essential to focus every nerve on the development of the situation. Upon receipt of the news, Foreign Minister Matsuoka went to the Imperial Palace, was received in audience and made the following report to The Throne.

"Now that war has begun between Germany and the Soviet Union, Japan should cooperate with Germany and attack the Soviet Union. For this purpose, Japan should refrain from taking action for the time being. Sooner or later we must fight. In the end, Japan will have to fight the Soviet Union, the United States, and Britain as our enemies." Of course, Matsuoka did not consult any Cabinet member but single-handedly took this action. His Majesty, seriously surprised at Matsuoka's remarks, summoned me at once for consultation. At the same time, through the Lord Keeper of the Privy Seal, Marquis Kido, His Majesty had the content of Matsuoka's talk communicated to me. By order of His Majesty, Matsuoka called on me at my home around 10:00 PM. What he said was not much clearer but it seemed that he told His Majesty his worst-case scenario prediction. The next day, June 23, when received in audience by the Emperor, I told His Majesty not to worry. I was in the dark as to whether Matsuoka's "strong views" represented his prediction or his insistence. Concerned about complications, I telephoned the Chief Secretary of the Cabinet from the Imperial Palace and ordered the scheduled liaison conference for that day to be canceled on account of the Reich-Soviet War.

In addition to His Majesty, Matsuoka also took similar information to Lord Keeper Kido and the people in general, causing scattered trouble. What I and Lord Keeper Kido ascertained was that Matsuoka insisted that the Soviet Union should be attacked and war with the U.S. avoided unless America participated in the war, in which case Japan would have to fight the U.S.

Though that was Matsuoka's view, to have the government attitude prevail, I had discussions with the Navy and War Ministers and also held a succession of liaison conferences on June 25, 26, 27, 28, 30 and July 1. On July 2, an Imperial Conference was held and the decision was made not to take action against the Soviet Union for the time being.

During the July 2 Imperial Conference, Matsuoka expressed very positive views. The Army had concentrated military strength in Manchuria and was prepared to begin a war with the Soviet Union for the chief purpose of checking the Army's action. As a result, somewhat in the sense of compensation, the advance into French Indo-China was recognized.

The situation was such that to check the Army's action and entirely refuse the Army's demand was calculated to invite a clash with the Army and not to resolve the issues. Moreover, in the American-Japanese negotiations then in progress, there was complete respect for compromise on the question of the advance into French Indo-China. In other words, we were confident in fully preventing the danger of war.

Matsuoka-Hull Duel

The United States attached importance to Japan's attitude toward the Reich-Soviet War. The American President ordered the Secretary of State to send a message directly to me on July 4 stating: "There is a report that Japan will take military action against the Soviet Union. Can't you assure us that this report is contrary to the truth?"

The message was communicated to me through Ambassador Joseph C. Grew on July 6. This was not customary. It provides proof of the United States' dislike of Matsuoka. I consulted the Foreign Minister and had him give Ambassador Grew, on July 8, a copy of a message Matsuoka handed to Ambassador Smetanin on July 2 as a reply to the American President's message. The occasion was used to ask the United States if the latter really intended to take part in the European War. On July 16, when the Cabinet resigned en bloc, the American reply said "Exercising the right of self-defense against Germany is only natural." The American reply was ironic in saying "A country which forces the United States to remain idle will be regarded as belonging to the factions of the countries bent on armed aggression."

Matsuoka then ended the prolonged dispute by expressing opposition to unrestricted abuse of the right of self-defense. He showed his dissatisfaction with a direct message being sent to me confidentially. Ambassador Grew, on the other hand, was quite evidently disappointed that a direct discussion with me was closed. The estrangement in relations between the Foreign Minister and Ambassador Grew went from bad to worse.

Konoye Sends Note to Foreign Minister on American-Japanese Relations Adjustment

Following the settlement of issues that arose when the German and Soviet War began, no further delay regarding American issues was tolerable nor could Matsuoka's vague attitude be ignored. Accordingly, on July 4, I sent him a letter communicating my views as follows:

1. Recourse to arms toward the South should not be made until the Northern issue has been settled. Efforts to adjust relations with the United States should be pursued. Army and Navy leaders have declared the virtual impossibility of Japan having both the U.S. and the Soviet Union as enemies. From this standpoint, advance into French Indo-China should be stopped, if possible.

2. As a result of the adjustment of relations with the U.S., it may be impossible to satisfy Germany's demand, leading to a possible unavoidable temporary chill in German-Japanese relations.

3. Adjustment of relations with the U.S. is necessary from the following standpoints.
   a) Increase of national power by acquiring goods and materials from areas overseas
   b) Prevention of Soviet-American rapprochement

    c)   Rapid promotion of peacemaking work with Chungking

4.   Based on these points, present negotiations with the U.S. should continue. Moreover, from the broader standpoint of national policy prosecution, a quick agreement should be sought.

In conclusion, I added the following passage:

"According to Your Excellency's far-sighted view, American-Japanese compromise may be impossible but I, as a man shouldering the heavy responsibility of assisting the Throne, can make only my best efforts, especially since His Majesty is seriously concerned about the matter. Now, we should do our best to have the negotiations materialize, even allowing a concession."

That evening, Foreign Minister Matsuoka telephoned his message to me stating that my letter inspired him. The following day he visited me at my official residence and declared the following: "In principle, I share the same view as the Prime Minister. Irrespective of public comment, I consider myself more enthusiastic than anyone else over the solution of American issues. It is absolutely untrue that I have regard for Germany's feelings. But should the Tripartite Pact get an opportunity on that account, I shall oppose it. Starting today, I shall consider the American issue in all seriousness. And if I am found to be an obstacle, I shall resign at any time." Such was Matsuoka's important statement.

Re-examination of Plan for American-Japanese Understanding

The discussion of the plan for American-Japanese understanding was to commence. On July 10 and 12, the liaison conferences were held to discuss the American plan of June 21. Its special features were:

1. In the item regarding the U.S. and Japanese governments' attitude toward the European War, the portion stating that both countries are to cooperate in attaining peace as proposed by Japan was eliminated. It was hinted that the U.S. would propel the drive to overthrow Germany.
2. Pertaining to Tripartite relations, it was to be clarified that Japan is to contribute to the prevention of extension of the European war due to non-provocation.

In making such a proposal, the U.S. was seen as trying to obtain a Japanese commitment to not engage in arms if the U.S. took part in the war as a result of German provocation.

1. Regarding the China issue, the distinction between the Chiang Kai-shek regime and the Nanking government was nullified in the first plan. It was simply stated that the U.S. would encourage the Chinese government to have peace with Japan. The Konoye Formula was mentioned but only the portion of it pertaining to good neigh-

bor friendship. Neither economic cooperation nor joint efforts to prevent Communism were mentioned. The U.S., seemingly apprehensive about public opinion, changed the terms to Japan's disadvantage.

2. The conditions of peace between Japan and China, which the Japanese once strongly desired, were restored as an addition, stating that a satisfactory agreement of views should be reached.

3. Whereas Japan proposed an American-Japanese economic agreement with the "Southwest" Pacific area to be covered, the U.S. revised it as covering the entire Pacific area.

Moreover, this plan was accompanied by an oral statement that the U.S. ardently hoped for the materialization of American-Japanese understanding and desired to have it more definitely confirmed that the Japanese government hoped the same. Thus, the oral statement tried to reflect the accurate Japanese insertions. One passage stated: "Among the influential Japanese government leaders, we find a man who has made an irrevocable commitment regarding the support of totalitarian Germany and its policy of conquest."

The American statement further stated that this fact was ascertained by information the American government obtained and, in that case, the understanding of the two countries now under consideration would prove "illusory" after all. This passage hinted at the criticism of Matsuoka. Suspicion also was expressed regarding stationing Japanese troops in China. Arrangements were made to have this June 21 plan discussed at the July 10 liaison conference.

My concerns were almost entirely neglected and Matsuoka became more uncompromising. He was distinctly inclined to oppose American-Japanese negotiations. At the July 10 liaison conference, he demanded the presence of Dr. Yoshio Saito, advisor to the Foreign Office and one of his henchmen. In the form of printed matter made available to those present, both men expressed a virtually wholesale opposition to American-Japanese negotiations. They claimed the U.S. proposal was inspired by a wicked motive to either conquer Japan or throw her into utter confusion. It was felt the oral statement, in particular, immediately should be returned to the U.S. and the American-Japanese negotiations disrupted. They asserted that the only remaining issues were the method and time.

Fighting Services Even Angered by Matsuoka

Seriously concerned about Matsuoka's strong attitude, I secretly conferred with the Ministers of Home Affairs, War and the Navy that same evening. At the July 12 liaison conference, the Army and Navy expressed joint views in contrast to those of Matsuoka.

1. Japan's attitude toward the European war shall be determined by treaty obligations and self-defense.

2. Regarding the China issue, the U.S. is to advise on a truce and peace based on the Three Principles of Prince Konoye, but the U.S. is not to intervene in the matter of peace conditions.

3. In case of need in the Pacific, the Empire reserves the right to exercise armed power.

The Army and Navy felt these points needed further clarification and no further objections to the American plan were necessary. They added that even if a rupture were to occur, it should be postponed until after Japan's advance into French Indo-China.

After all, Foreign Minister Matsuoka agreed to the preparation of our counter-plan based on the Army and Navy's views. Following the end of the discussion, talks ensued among Director Muto of the Naval Affairs Bureau, Director Terasaki of the American Bureau of the Foreign Office, Chief Secretary Somita of the Cabinet and Advisor Saito of the Foreign Office and resulted in the draft of a so-called final plan.

The only remaining question to be settled was obtaining Matsuoka's consent of the draft plan. Despite the Army and Navy's urgently repeated requests, he refused to see the plan on the pretext of illness. Meanwhile, it was discovered that he had seen the German Ambassador and others, causing the Army and Navy's indignation. On July 12, Advisor Saito's explanation was heard and the final plan, with Matsuoka's revised views interwoven, was completed. Though it took only one or two days, the prevailing attitude in government circles was hostile and the political situation became very tense.

Due to Matsuoka's revisions, the counter-proposal, as drafted by the Japanese side, differed from the June 21 American plan on the following points:

1. The section pertaining to the common efforts of Japan and the U.S. for an early conclusion of the European war was restored with the attached condition: "... when a proper time comes...", so that the American side might accept this.

2. The portion concerning Tripartite Pact relations was revised, i.e. "... in case of extension of the European war, the Japanese government will determine its attitude only in consideration of its treaty obligations and the defense and safety of its own country".

3. In the section pertaining to the China issue, the Konoye Principles were praised and the name of "the Nanking government", toward which the U.S. was averse, was avoided. It was clearly stated that the U.S. was to advise the Chiang regime on peace.

4. The terms of Sino-Japanese peace was again erased.

5. On the grounds of needed American-Japanese economic cooperation, especially in the Southwest Pacific, the entire Pacific area was again revised to "Southwest Pacific."

Foreign Minister Again Acts Willfully

Now that this plan was completed after much effort, everyone thought it would be sent to the U.S. at once. However, Matsuoka opined that instruction should first be cabled to Washington for refusing to accept the oral statement. Branding the oral statement as a rude and improper document, the instructions stated that unless the American government withdrew it, Japan was in no position to discuss further an American-Japanese understanding. The Army, Navy and I feared that if these instructions alone were sent, it would serve only to hurt the feelings of the Americans and might lead to a rupture. Thus, we strongly insisted that both the instructions and the Japanese plan could be sent together.

Matsuoka ignored the arrangement made between him and me through Advisor Saito and had the instructions regarding the refusal of the oral statement cabled at 11:30 PM on July 14. Secretary of State Hull was surprised at the manner in which his oral statement was received and interpreted in Japan. On July 17 he withdrew it to dispel misunderstanding. On July 15, Matsuoka ordered Director Sakamoto of the Foreign Office European-Asiatic Affairs Bureau to show him confidentially the final Japanese plan for the Germans, a plan which had not yet been communicated to the U.S.

The Shift of Foreign Minister Abandoned

At this juncture, not only I but other Cabinet Ministers felt it was no longer possible to dispose of an important diplomatic issue under the prevailing condition. At the July 15 Cabinet meeting from which Matsuoka was absent, I discussed the situation with the Home, War, and Navy Ministers. The War Minister said:

"Dismissing the Foreign Minister would cause a negative effect and, though we have continued our efforts to cooperate with him, things have arrived at a point where it is no longer possible. We have to either dismiss the Foreign Minister or resign en bloc."

The four Ministers agreed. If Matsuoka alone was to be dismissed, serious waves might ensue from the standpoint of his strong position that, i.e., "The U.S.'s oral statement is an attempt to force a reorganization of the Japanese Cabinet." The Ministers also expressed that aside from the question of the Foreign Minister or the American issue, the basis for the general resignation should be strengthening the war structure. The meeting adjourned with agreement to continue the discussion the next day.

I went to the Hayama Detached Palace at 2:00 PM and reported to The Throne. His Majesty asked, "Isn't it possible to let go of Matsuoka alone?" I replied that after thinking over the issue, I would make the best of it but, given the present condition, further existence of the Cabinet was impossible. I then met the Lord Keeper of the Privy Seal and shared the reason for which we had to resign en bloc, adding "Home Minister Hiranuma should be the next Premier." The Lord Keeper neither said yes nor no, but said that I should take action without delay.

Cabinet Resigns en Bloc

In accordance with the previous day's arrangements, at noon on July 16, the Premier, Home Minister, War and Navy Ministers and the President of the Planning Board confidentially conferred at the detached house at Mejiro and decided to resign en bloc. Following proper arrangements made by the Secretary of the Cabinet, I suddenly called an extraordinary Cabinet session and collected the resignation papers of the Cabinet Ministers for submission to the Throne. Matsuoka was absent due to illness and the Chief Secretary of the Cabinet went to his home and obtained his resignation paper. Matsuoka seemed distinctly surprised and highly dissatisfied by the decision that favored general resignation. Unable to resist the decision, he entrusted his seal impression to the Chief Secretary. At 8:50 that evening, I went to Hayama again and submitted the Cabinet's resignation. Returning to Tokyo at 11:00 PM, I reported to the Cabinet Ministers that the life of the second Konoye Cabinet was ended.

Imperial Order for Reorganization of Cabinet

At 5:10 PM on July 17, by commanded to go to the Imperial Palace, I received the Imperial order to form another Cabinet. By 5:30 PM the next afternoon that was completed, I presented the list of Cabinet members to The Throne at 7:00 PM. At 8:50 PM, we were installed and the third newly formed Konoye Cabinet had its first meeting at 9:45 PM. Notable was the inclusion of Admiral Teijiro Toyoda as Foreign Minister.

I recommended Admiral Toyoda for the foreign portfolio because of my strong desire to have the American-Japanese negotiations materialize in some way. Admiral Toyoda had served as Vice-Minister of the Navy, was well versed in Navy affairs and had recently served as Minister of Commerce and Industry, handling various issues pertaining to goods and materials. He supported the view that an American-Japanese conflict should be avoided as much as circumstances permitted.

This significant political change was not clear to the Japanese Ambassador Admiral Kichisaburo Nomura in Washington. Because he and his staff failed to understand the significance of the Cabinet change, nothing was done to communicate its significance to the Americans. The Tokyo government hoped the new Cabinet organization would favorably impress the U.S., speed up negotiations and clarify the vague atmosphere. Regrettably, this did not occur. In spite of the fact that the Japanese counter-proposal plan to the June 21 U.S. plan was laboriously and painfully prepared, it was not shown to the Americans despite July 15 instructions to do so. Failure to submit the plan was due to two reasons, i.e., the Cabinet change and fear the Japanese plan would be unacceptable to the U.S. The non-submission of the plan became clear from reading the July 22 telegram from Ambassador Nomura. Moreover, on July 23, he displayed his ignorance by requesting instructions, stating "American policy of new cabinet to be shown in haste."

Things Go Against My Will

As seen in the foregoing, the Japanese Cabinet's enthusiasm in handling U.S.-Japan negotiations was not conveyed to the Americans at all, while the time for the Japanese advance into French Indo-China, as previously decided in the Cabinet meeting, approached. As military movements in the South Pacific became active, the American government's suspicion became too obvious to conceal. As reported in Ambassador Nomura's July 24 telegram to Tokyo, the U.S. grew to believe Japan conveyed to the Axis Powers that adjusting U.S.-Japan relations was a scheme to be used until the completion of preparations for advancement into the Southern area. In Japan, on the other hand, the words "the encirclement line against Japan" became frequently used. On the whole, the press carried articles of anti-American views admittedly contrary to the Cabinet's will.

On July 21, Undersecretary of State Welles, in place of Secretary of State Hull who was ill, sent for Minister

Kaname Wakasugi as a representative of Ambassador Nomura and warned the latter as follows: "According to the formation, indications are that Japan intends to capture French Indo-China. Should that happen, negotiations at that point would be of no use."

In his conference with Nomura on July 23, Undersecretary of State Welles presented the following important representation. "Heretofore, the United States has been negotiating with Japan with great perseverance, but now the foundation is lost." The following day, Nomura informally spoke with President Roosevelt when the latter pointed out the Indo-China issue to be an important question and made the following proposal:

1. On the condition that the Japanese troops withdraw from French Indo-China (if Japanese troops have already moved there)
2. Joint guarantee of the neutralization of Indo-China by Japan, U.S., Britain, Holland, and China
3. Guarantee of acquisition of materials from French Indo-China

Thus, on July 26, the Tokyo government announced one after the other, the Japanese advancement into Indo-China and the U.S. government's announcement of the Japanese Freezing Assets Decree. In view of the aggravating situation, that night I sent for the Chief of the Metropolitan Police Board and ordered him to have the American Embassy guarded.

America Fails to Agree to our Re-Proposition

From ten days from prior to or after the political change to the advance of Japanese troops into French Indo-China, there were seen many desirable points in bringing Washington and Tokyo to a mutually good understanding. However, the impression was that the U.S.-Japan peace talks had completely failed. The Cabinet maintained hope to the last and made efforts to resume negotiations, taking advantage of Roosevelt's proposal relating to French Indo-China as proposed on July 24. Extending this proposal, on July 31 Undersecretary of State Welles handed to the Japanese an additional proposal advocating Thailand's neutralization.

Successive conferences were held in Tokyo on July 29 and 30 and August 2 and 4. I spoke with Navy and Finance Ministers on July 31 and with the War Minister on August 1. I made every conceivable effort to cope with the situation by conversing with Mitsuru Toyama and others, and I also sought an understanding with the rightwing elements.

At an August 4 liaison conference, it was decided to approach the U.S. with a proposal. The same proposal was in the form of a reply to President Roosevelt's proposal, but it was designed to serve as a key for resuming U.S.-Japan negotiations which were deadlocked. Its principle was:

1. Japan has no intention of advancing her troops beyond French Indo-China and will withdraw troops from Indo-China after the China affair settlement.
2. Philippine neutrality shall be guaranteed.
3. The U.S. shall disarm herself in the Southwest Pacific area.
4. The U.S. shall help Japan obtain resources in the Dutch East Indies.
5. The U.S. shall render its good offices for direct negotiations to be held between the Republic of China and Japan and, additionally, shall recognize Japan's special position in French Indo-China even after the latter's withdrawal of troops from Indo-China.

The foregoing instructions were dispatched to Ambassador Nomura on August 5 who gave them to Secretary of State Hull on August 6. However, Hull failed to show any interest in our proposal, emphasizing there was no room for the resumption of U.S.-Japan negotiations unless Japan gave up her saber-rattling policy.

Ambassador Nomura reported that indications pointed to the U.S. being prepared for any eventuality. On August 8, Hull gave America's reply to Nomura which failed to touch on the content of Japan's proposal and pointed out that, as printed, it failed to address the point of the President's proposal. Hull was very indifferent, repeating the President's proposal in only one or two words.

Determination to see the President

Racking my brain for removing the deadlock in American-Japanese relations, I finally determined to see the American President. I revealed my intention for the first time on August 4 to the War and Navy Ministers as follows:

1. I consider it our duty to do the best under the circumstances. There have been various misunderstandings in the American-Japanese negotiations and indications that the true intentions of both parties have not been communicated to each other. Should this be allowed to continue unchecked, and should we plunge into war, as statesmen, we should have no apology to offer to the people in general and to His Majesty who is highly concerned over American-Japanese relations and world peace.

    If we do our best and yet war begins, we cannot help it. In that event, our determination and that of the people will be firm. Prior to the outbreak of the European War, Chamberlain went to the continent several times to see Hitler and, although he was deceived by Hitler, I believe Chamberlain's visits had a positive effect on the British people's determination.

2. Present this is a touch-and-go crisis. Negotiations through Ambassador Nomura will be closely monitored. The Prime Minister should see the

President and forthrightly and boldly acquaint him with our true intentions. If the President fails to understand us, the Prime Minister will, of course, leave the meeting. If direct talks fail, people will understand that an American-Japanese war was inevitable and be even more determined. The outside world will see that Japan was not bent on aggression but displayed sincerity for the maintenance of peace in the Pacific. To a certain extent, this probably will relieve the irritation of international public opinion.

3. The President's visit to Honolulu is not impossible since it was mentioned in the original plan of understanding. Moreover, hope should not be initially abandoned. The U.S. maintains its stand based on the Nine Power Pact and the views of two parties do agree. The U.S. says "The United States is prepared to be consulted at any time regarding revision of the Nine Power Pact by a reasonable and legitimate method."

4. This discussion needs to commence quickly because it appears the Reich-Soviet War will reach its peak in September. If the war deadlocks, as some predict, Germany's future will not be optimistic. In that case, the U.S. will maintain a stronger attitude and not bother talking with Japan. Even if Germany gains an advantage in the Reich-Soviet War, it will not cause Japan any

significant disadvantage. It is possible that Germany's feeling toward Japan may cool down but Germany's hegemony or complete victory over Britain and the U.S. is unthinkable, and ways to adjust German-Japanese relations will be found.

5. Accordingly, there is no need for us to be concerned about Germany developing an advantage in the Reich-Soviet War. Rather, we should fully consider the case of a disadvantaged Germany and reach some understanding with the U.S. now.

6. However, this does not mean that any arrangement with the U.S., with whom we should not curry favor or yield in haste for some understanding or arrangement, would be acceptable. In short, we must do all we can and do our best both domestically and externally under the circumstances.

Navy and Army Support Conditionally

The War and Navy Ministers listened to me with tense looks. They could not reply on the spot but the naval side expressed its wholesale approval of my proposal within the day, adding the Navy was looking forward to the conference with anticipation. The War Minister's reply came in the form of a document:

"The Prime Minister's interview with the American President is calculated to inevitably weaken the present diplomacy of the Empire based on the Tripartite Alliance and is considered likely to cause considerable waves domestically. Accordingly, such an interview is considered improper. However, given the present pressing situation, the Prime Minister personally proposes trying to remove the deadlock, a determination highly respected by the Army. If the Prime Minister intends to attend the conference by adhering to the fundamental policy of the revised Japanese plan and leave the meeting, determined to wage war on the U.S. if the American President fails to understand Japan's real intentions and means to carry out the present policy, the Army will not object to the Prime Minister's direct discussion with the President."

The Army's Document Accompanied by the Following Annex

"If the forthcoming meeting is to be arranged between our Prime Minister and Secretary of State Hull or any other officials except President Roosevelt, the Army will oppose it. If the conference should fail, the Prime Minister should not resign but rather bolster his determination to take the initiative for an American-Japanese War." The War Minister also thought the possibility of failure was greater than that of success regarding the conference. The concluding view was that the matter should be expedited.

On August 6, immediately after the liaison conference, I was received in the audience by the Emperor and
revealed my intention and determination to The Throne.
The following day I was summoned to the Imperial Palace and urged by His Majesty to quickly pursue my proposal, saying: "We have heard from the Navy concerning
the total prohibition of American oil exports to Japan
and your interview with the President should be done
without any loss of time."

Instructions in this regard were sent to Ambassador
Nomura on August 7. The initial impression given by
the American side was exceedingly disappointing. The
President was absent from Washington for an interview
with Premier Churchill. On August 8, Nomura met Hull
and gave him the proposal. Hull said that as long as
there was no change in Japan's policy, he was not confident about introducing it to the President. Nomura said
nothing further and cabled that Ambassador Grew
should be approached in Tokyo.

In the U.S., a joint statement was issued by President
Roosevelt and Premier Churchill, generating very cut-
ting comments by some of the Tokyo press which was
cabled. Moreover, an attempt on State Minister Hiranuma's life on August 14 was highly sensationalized. True
to America's traditional diplomacy of what needs doing
should be done irrespective of the occasion, on August
13, Hull handed Nomura a protest mentioning alleged
violations of American rights and interests in China. The
American Cabinet Ministers with whom Nomura dealt
pessimistically felt the U.S. should not consent to have a

meeting of leaders, the success of which was uncertain. Sensing the urgently important situation, prior to the President's return to the White House, Nomura met with Hull again to explain the true intentions of our side. As usual, Hull simply repeated his opposition to "military domination." However, he somewhat softened his attitude regarding a proposed meeting with the President, saying "If you have full confidence of success, I shall introduce the plan to the White House."

President in Good Humor

Suddenly, on August 17, after his mid-ocean talk, President Roosevelt invited Ambassador Nomura and made two representations. One warned against a further armed advance of Japan. The other was a reply to the proposal for the two countries' leaders to meet. According to his talk, the American government appreciated my and the Japanese government's idea and, in principle, expressed approval saying: "If the Japanese government halts its expansion activities and hopes to move toward peace in the Pacific as well as a program and principles which the U.S. has pledged and promised, the U.S. will be prepared to re-open the unofficial negotiations which were interrupted in July. Moreover, the U.S. gladly will try to exchange views with Japan and arrange the time and place for such a meeting." In the end, the President required a clear-cut statement to be submitted for that purpose.

The peace program would comprise:

- economic opportunity, applying the principle of equal treatment throughout the Pacific area
- voluntary and peaceful cooperation of the Pacific area's inhabitants
- assistance to people subject to menace
- removal of military or political control of monopolistic or priority economic rights

Throughout the Roosevelt-Nomura talk, the American President was in good humor, even saying: "As the meeting place, Hawaii, is geographically improper and Juneau in Alaska would be fitting, what do you say to have the talk in mid-October?"

It also was learned from one of the Cabinet Ministers whom Ambassador Nomura met that President Roosevelt took the issue from the routine official's hands and intended to seek a solution from a broader standpoint. Nomura cabled Tokyo stating that the present opportunity should not be missed and that bold responses should be made. As a reference, he cabled to us his own private planned reply to the President.

On August 18, Foreign Minister Toyoda invited Ambassador Grew, dwelt on the reasons for which the interview between the two leaders was needed and requested his influence in making that happen.

Hull's Attitude Pessimistic

Our reply to the American representation as given to Ambassador Nomura by President Roosevelt on August 17 was determined at the liaison conference on August 26. Along with the reply, the conference also adopted a message I prepared for presentation to the American President. My message clearly stated my true intentions for having proposed the conference with President Roosevelt to discuss American-Japanese affairs from a broader standpoint without adhering to routine discussions and thus coping with the rapidly changing situation.

On August 28, Ambassador Nomura gave these two documents to President Roosevelt. After praising the message as splendid, he said "I should like to have a discussion with Prince Konoye for about three days. Although he did not initiate a meeting time, he showed great interest in the proposal. Perhaps this was the time when Japan and the United States were the closest to rapprochement.

In contrast to the President, who was very interested in the proposed conference, Secretary of State Hull was extremely cautious. Hull, who was with Roosevelt when the Ambassador called, invited Nomura to a discussion and made it clear that his views fundamentally differed from those of the Japanese, and repeated American insistence that "The leaders' meeting should be made in the form of ratification of a talk previously established."

Nomura's report on the optimistic atmosphere in which Roosevelt received our documents and on the pessimistic Hull were received here on August 29 and 30. The report reflected an important suggestion regarding the deadlock. The Japanese government's observations were divided between optimistic and pessimistic. However, to handle the proposed conference, both the Army and Navy began selecting their representatives for the conference. The Foreign Office was more or less optimistic, anticipating the "political" solution of the President to the neglect of the State Department's traditional diplomatic reasoning. At the August 30 liaison conference, Foreign Minister Toyoda was extremely optimistic.

President's Attitude Changes

On September 3, President Roosevelt confidentially invited Ambassador Nomura and handed him a reply to the "Konoye Message." Although couched in courteous language, Roosevelt's reply evaded a clear cut expression regarding his agreement to the proposed conference. Moreover, it stated the necessity of obtaining Japan's agreement regarding the fundamental principles as the pre-condition. It was made clear that the State Department's view had taken control of the situation.

Separate Proposal to the United States

On September 3, the day of the Nomura-Roosevelt discussion, a separate proposal to the U.S., drafted by the Foreign Office was being discussed at the liaison conference in Tokyo. It was a simplification of the plan for understanding discussed between Nomura and Hull under a different premise. The proposed plan was:

1. Japan shall not advance troops beyond French Indo-China.
2. Japan's interpretation of the Tripartite Pact shall be done autonomously.
3. Japan shall withdraw troops from China in accordance with the terms of the Sino-Japanese Pact.
4. The economic activities of the United States in China shall not be restricted as long as they are conducted on a fair basis.
5. The principle of equal treatment in commerce and trade in the Southwest Pacific shall be established.
6. Steps shall be taken for the restoration of legitimate trade and commercial relations between Japan and the United States.

The Foreign Office's great deal of hope regarding this plan was communicated to Ambassador Grew from Foreign Minister Toyoda and to Secretary of State Hull from Ambassador Nomura. The plan did not represent any new proposal but aimed to deal with concrete issues which were considered urgent at that time and make them the basis of the leaders' talks. Contrary to the Foreign Office's usual anticipation, the September 4 plan simply invited unnecessary misunderstanding and chaos.

The U.S. was not unreasonable in entertaining the misunderstanding, for the June 21 plan submitted by the U.S. to Japan had remained unanswered although our reply had been sent to Washington on July 15. Nomura failed to deliver our reply to the U.S. plan which was offered as a final one. As far as the U.S. was concerned, they had received the September 4 plan without receiving a reply to its June 21 plan. I consider this the major reason responsible for the American misunderstanding.

While such complex ongoing diplomatic negotiations were being conducted between Tokyo and Washington, a serious issue arose in our government circles in Tokyo, i.e., to what extent should we continue negotiations with the U.S.? Should we give it up, give up hope and fight the United States?

Secret Negotiations Leak Out

The American-Japanese talks were made known only to the government leaders. Among them, only Foreign Minister Matsuoka opposed them. Out of fear of opposition from the lower strata, the talks were kept confidential but knowledge of them began to leak. With Matsuoka's confidential sharing of the talks with the Italo-German side as the turning point, the public became vaguely aware. Opposition arose from both the lower strata and the Army. The Japanese people were shocked to learn of the start of the Reich-Soviet War. Government leaders controlled opinions in favor of immediate commencement of war against the Soviet Union but had to adopt the Cabinet's decision in favor of an advance into French Indo-China as a form of compensation.

The advance of troops into French Indo-China had immediate and strong effects. The U.S. severed economic relations with Japan and announced that its traditional policy alone was peace. Nearing the end of August, the "national policy" of plunging into war with Britain and the U.S. was discussed at liaison and other conferences.

Basic Principles of Prosecution of National Policy Determined

On September 6 an Imperial Conference was held during which the following "basic principles of the prosecution of the national policy of the Empire" were determined. I stated that in view of the present pressing situation, the offensives of the U.S., Britain, the Netherlands, and others toward Japan and the flexibility of the Empire's national power, the enforcement of measures regarding the Southern regions shall be made as follows:

1. The Empire shall complete war preparations within the last decade of October determining not to mind a war with the United States (Britain and the Netherlands) for the purpose of guaranteeing its self-existence and self-defense.

2. Parallel to it, the Empire shall have recourse to diplomatic means in dealing with the United States and Britain and endeavor to have its demands attained.

3. If still no way is found for the attainment of our demands, even in the first half of October, the Empire shall immediately determine to commence war with the United States (Britain and the Netherlands). Policies other than the Southern policies shall remain unchanged and attempts shall be made to prevent American-Soviet understanding or establishment of a joint front.

His Majesty Insists on Peace

One day prior to the Imperial Conference, I proceeded to the Imperial Palace and submitted a report to The Throne regarding the basic principles of national policy. His Majesty said: "Seeing this report, I am impressed by the fact that it puts first importance on war preparations, and diplomacy is calculated to let one think that diplomacy is subservient to armed power. About these points, I shall question the two Chiefs of the General Staff and Naval General Staff at tomorrow's meeting."

I replied to His Majesty: "The order of A and B does not have any degree of importance. The government intends to conduct diplomatic negotiations to the last and, in case they are not successful, we shall have to make war preparations."

I further said: "It may be improper for Your Majesty to pose such a question at tomorrow's Imperial Conference. If Your Majesty desires to pose a question to the members of the Supreme Command, Your Majesty should summon them at once."

His Majesty ordered the Chiefs of the Army and Navy General Staff to be summoned at once and ordered me to be present. When General Gen Sugiyama, Chief of the Army General Staff and Admiral Osami Nagano, Chief of the Naval General Staff came, His Majesty asked Sugiyama:

"In case of an American-Japanese conflict, how many months does the Army consider with confidence it will take to dispose of the matter?"

Sugiyama replied: "As far as the Southern area is concerned, we intend to settle things during the first three months."

His Majesty further asked Sugiyama: "At the time of the China Affair outbreak, you were the War Minister and, in that capacity, I remember you said 'The Affair will be settled within a month or so.' And yet the Affair has lasted four years and not been settled."

Awestruck, Sugiyama explained that China had a large area in the hinterland and offered various explanations at length. His Majesty then addressed Sugiyama: "If you say China has a wide hinterland, the Pacific Ocean is larger, isn't it? With what confidence do you say it will take three months?"

Sugiyama lowered his head and failed to reply. At that point, Chief Nagano of the Naval General Staff came to Sugiyama's rescue. "Representing the High Command, I shall offer an explanation from a broader standpoint. If American-Japanese relations are likened to a patient, the patient now stands at the crossroads of whether he should undergo an operation or not. If left alone, the patient may slowly weaken but, if he undergoes an operation, though seriously risky, there may be hope for recovery. The High Command hopes that a solution will be attained through diplomatic means but in case of failure, an operation will have to be conducted. In this sense, we approve the proposal."

His Majesty was emphatic in asking: "I understand the High Command today puts major importance on diplomacy. Is that true?"

Both Chiefs of the High Command replied that his Majesty was right.

On the occasion of the Imperial Conference held the following morning, September 6 at 10 AM, Baron Dr. Yoshimichi Hara, President of the Privy Council, spoke: "I am impressed by the fact that, in the proposed plan, importance is placed on war rather than diplomacy. I would like a clarification of the government and High Command's views." The Navy Minister representing the government spoke, but no member of the High Command spoke.

Suddenly, His Majesty addressed the gathering. "The question now posed by President Hara of the Privy Council is quite reasonable and I exceedingly regret that no reply whatsoever has been made by the High Council." Then His Majesty removed from his pocket a piece of paper on which his grandfather, Emperor Meiji, had composed this poem:

"Though I consider the surrounding seas as my brothers, why is it that the waves should rise so high?"

Reading the poem aloud, His Majesty said: "I always read and appreciate this poem and am endeavoring to live up to the spirit of the Great Emperor who was so fond of peace."

What consistent logic! For several minutes, no one dared to speak.

Then Chief Nagano of the Naval General Staff rose and spoke: "I am filled with awe at the censure Your Majesty has given to the High Command. I thought when the Navy Minister replied, he represented both the government and the High Command. The High Command, as the Navy Minister replied, places major importance on diplomatic negotiations and would appeal to arms only in an unavoidable situation."

Thus, the Imperial Conference adjourned amid an unprecedentedly tense atmosphere.

Secret Talk with Ambassador Grew

At one time, American-Japanese negotiations for understanding appeared to be progressing rapidly but at another, they seemed to be blocked. The proposal for a meeting of the leaders interested the American President and yet it failed to materialize. I thought this state of affairs was due to the Japanese making their real intentions known to the Americans through cabled instructions to Ambassador Nomura alone. Thus, I determined to see what I could accomplish by seeing Ambassador Grew personally.

On September 6, the day the "basic principles of national policy" were determined, with the understanding of the War, Navy and Foreign Ministers, I conferred with the Ambassador Grew in utter secrecy. With Counselor Douman as interpreting, we dined and talked. I stressed that my Cabinet with the Army and Navy united was hoping for successful negotiations and that no better opportunity would be forthcoming.

Then I made a very significant declaration: "If we miss this chance, another will not come in our lifetime."

I also revealed that the Army, Navy, and Foreign Office had virtually completed selecting their delegations and dwelt on the necessity of me seeing the President and exchanging views with him on fundamental issues as soon as circumstances permitted. Ambassador Grew ascertained my views regarding the four basic principles of Secretary of State Hull, and I said:

"Basically, they are all right but, in the sense of actual operation, various issues will arise and for resolving them, our interview with the President is necessary."

Following a 90 minute talk, Ambassador Grew promised to report the contents of the day's interview directly to the President. Significantly impressed by the import of my message, Grew remarked:

"This report will become the most important cable I ever file with my home government since I began my diplomatic career."

Question of Stationing Troops a Hard Nut to Crack

Although I gave my best efforts to the success of the negotiations, the important national policy determined at the September 6 Imperial Conference had a time limit to negotiations. The impression was strongly felt that the final stage had arrived.

By that time, the difficult points of the negotiations were virtually grasped and the intentions of the American government also were generally understood. Basically, the U.S. adhered to the "four principles" and, concretely, the country raised the question of stationing troops, the question of economy and equal opportunity, and the Tripartite Pact.

The Americans believed that Japan had no objections to the four principles and I also declared to the American Ambassador that, in principle, they were acceptable. Thus, no special issues appeared unlikely to rise, but strong opposing views, even in principle, did not die out in the Army and a section of the Foreign Office. There was the persistent argument that, since the U.S. interpreted Japan's August 28 representation in the foregoing sense due to Ambassador Nomura's mistranslation, a representation should be made for a retraction or the Ambassador should be recalled. If the denial was to be made at this time, even for the four basic principles, American-Japanese negotiations would surely be totally wrecked. Therefore, I seriously considered how to address the issue.

Regarding the economic principles, Japan already was determined to recognize an equal opportunity in China. The view was optimistic that little trouble would be encountered since the U.S. had a clear awareness of Japan's special geographical relation to China. As for the Tripartite Act issue, it was thought, although any promise could not be documented, if I met the President, some agreement might be attained.

Regarding stationing troops in China, the Army first said that the name or form would not matter, but the next day that moderate view was replaced, i.e., that the Army's position was absolutely immutable. Within the Japanese government, there was a strong impression that stationing troops were the biggest issue.

Because of the serious thrust of the basic national policy determined by the September 6 Imperial Conference on the progress of American-Japanese negotiations, government leaders continued to feel severely distressed. I often stopped overnight in the Japanese room of my official residence. On September 24 and 25, I continued lengthy conferences with the War, Navy and Foreign Ministers and the President of the Planning Board.

From September 27 to October 1, I rested at Kamakura but, in the meantime, I invited Navy Minister Oikawa to a discussion and listened to the Navy's prevailing views. On October 4, I went to the Imperial Palace and was received in audience by His Majesty. Later I ordered bureau chiefs to leave me and I held a liaison conference with the Cabinet Ministers and High Command leaders. The next evening, I invited the War Minister to my home at Ogikubo and expressed my determination to continue my negotiations with the U.S. to the last.

Late on the night of October 7, the War Minister called on me at the Japanese room of the Official Residence and made the following strong stand: "In regard to the question of stationing troops, the Army absolutely is unable to accept a formula of basically total withdrawal and then station troops."

In view of the Army and Navy's strong attitude, I had individual talks with the Navy Minister and Foreign Minister on October 6 and 8 and discussed the matter of staving off the crisis. On October 10, the Foreign Minister called on me and we discussed the continuation of talks with the U.S. Another liaison conference occurred on October 11. Meanwhile, the activities of the big three Secretaries of the Cabinet, especially President Suzuki of the Planning Board, became the object of attention.

Navy Entrusts Matter of War or Peace to Prime Minister

On October 12, marking my 50th birthday, in spite of it being Sunday, I invited the War, Navy and Foreign Affairs Ministers and also Planning Board President Suzuki to my private home at Ogikubo and held what was virtually the last conference on peace or war. Prior to the conference, the following report was made to the Chief Secretary of the Cabinet from the Naval Affairs Bureau of the Navy Office:

"The Navy does not desire to have American-Japanese negotiations disrupted and desires to avoid war as much as circumstances permit. But the Navy cannot openly say it. At today's conference, the Navy Minister will propose 'entrusting to the Prime Minister the matter of deciding choosing either peace or war.' Please understand this point."

As expected, the Navy Minister spoke first at the conference as outlined in the following:

"Now the time has come to choose either war or peace. We should like to entrust the matter to the Prime Minister. If peace is to be maintained, it should be maintained throughout. In other words, even by making a concession to some extent, we should let the negotiations materialize. If after two or three months, there is a failure, if war is chosen, the Navy will be troubled. If war is to be resorted to, we should make the decision at once. Now is the time for us to decide either way. If war is to be avoided, we want to have you continue the negotiations with the goal of attaining success."

Replying to the Navy Minister's statement, I said: "If a decision is to be made today, I favor the continuation of the negotiations."

The War Minister then replied: "That conclusion of the Prime Minister is premature. It would be serious if we continued the hopeless negotiations and, thus, miss the opportunity. Does the Foreign Minister have any confidence of success in the negotiations?"

The Foreign Minister replied: "That depends on the conditions. I think the greatest difficulty now confronting us is the questions of stationing troops in China. If the Army is averse to making the slightest concession, the negotiations have no hope of success. If the Army doesn't mind a concession on that issue, I can't say there absolutely is no hope for success in the negotiations."

The War Minister said: "The question of stationing troops is the very life of the Army and absolutely no concession can be given."

I said: "If we give up form and take the substance, it will be alright. In other words, if we follow the form insisted on by the U.S. but, in substance, attain results similar to stationing troops, it will be alright, won't it?"

The War Minister would not consent to my proposal. The conference lasted from 2:00 to 6:00 PM and adjourned without reaching a conclusion.

War Minister Unyielding

The following day, October 13, I went to the Imperial Palace and reported to his Majesty the critical situation confronting the Cabinet. I also conferred with the Lord Keeper of the Privy Seal and at 9:00 AM on October 14, I called the War Minister to my official residence, prior to the Cabinet meeting, and requested him to reconsider the matter of stationing troops.

I said: "I have a serious responsibility for the China Affair which has lasted four years and has not yet been concluded. I cannot agree to plunge into a great war whose outcome is uncertain. At this point, we should temporarily yield to the U.S., let the country have its form of troop withdrawal, and stave off the danger of an American-Japanese war. I also consider it necessary to bring the China Affair to a conclusion, which would add to the rational power of this country. While the development of national fortunes is desirable, in order to obtain great expansion, it is often necessary to yield to others and build national power.

The War Minister disagreed, saying: "If we yield to the U.S. now, they will become more arrogant and overbearing. Regarding troop withdrawal, you say the name shall be abandoned and the substance is taken, but I disagree from the standpoint of maintaining morale." The talk with the War Minister was unproductive and, when the Cabinet conference began, he vociferously dwelt on the reasons for discontinuing American-Japanese negotiations.

All Recklessly at Stake

During the talks I had with the War Minister, the following was said: "Sometimes it is necessary to close one's eyes and jump from the stage of the Kiyomizu Temple." The chance may come once or twice in a lifetime. But when consideration is given to the 2,600-year-old national policy and the 100,000,000 people, no such thing can be done by anyone in a responsible position."

There had been many references to such expressions as "staking all" or "staking the national fortunes."

Foreign Minister Matsuoka frequently used such expressions but every time I heard such expressions, the feeling was unpleasant. For some, the use of such expressions may be exhilarating but, when one considers the untainted 2,600-year-old national policy, one cannot lightly plunge into a war with an uncertain outcome. This is entirely different from an individual's case. People may call me hesitant or temporizing, but I cannot undertake such a reckless adventure. However roundabout it may be, I am confident that the course to be followed must be 100 percent safe and war avoided.

Some soldiers say "Japan does not have a 100 percent chance of victory in either the Sino-Japanese or Russo-Japanese War."

In discussion with the War Minister, referring to the foregoing statement by some soldiers, I said:

"I think Ito and Yamagata were fully confident in undertaking the Russo-Japanese War. It would be outrageous if they did so without full confidence of victory. Prior to the outbreak of that War, Emperor Meiji had not made a decision. When Premier Katsura desired the Emperor's decision, Prince Ito stopped him and asked him to allow one more day for him to think it over. The next morning, the Emperor summoned Prince Ito and asked if he felt confident of victory. The Prince replied that, at least, the Russians will be unable to set a single foot in Korea and we will be able to keep the Russian troops beyond the Yalu River for a least a year. While maintaining this position for a year or so, mediation by third or more power may be expected. Of the third powers, Britain is our ally while France and Germany side with Russia. We can depend only on the United States. If we take action, we are confident about the results. This was the advice given to The Throne. The Emperor's anxiety was relieved and His Majesty decided in favor of war at the Imperial Conference held the same day. However, this time there were no third powers. No one is in a position to mediate and the future looks utterly uncertain. We must be very cautious about plunging into such an uncertain war."

During the last talk at my official residence on October 14, the War Minister said: "I think the Prime Minister's views are too pessimistic. You know our vulnerability too well. Isn't it true that the U.S. has its own vulnerability?"

That day's discussion resulted in what one may call a frontal clash regarding the question of troop withdrawal. At the discussion's end, the War Minister said impressively "This is a matter of difference in character."

The War Minister's statement at the October 14 Cabinet meeting was very sudden and not a single Cabinet member responded. Other agenda items were discussed and the meeting adjourned without addressing Tojo's remarks.

Tojo Advises General Resignation

The same afternoon, Director Muto of the War Office Military Affairs Bureau told the Chief Secretary of the Cabinet: "It seems to us that the Prime Minister remains indecisive because the Navy doesn't make up its mind. If the Navy really does not want war, the Army must consider it. But the Navy does not say that openly and says it has entrusted the matter to the Prime Minister. The

Prime Minister's decision alone would fail to control the Army men. If the Navy officially tells the Army, 'The Navy at this time doesn't want war', the Army will easily control their men. Can't the Cabinet take action to induce the Navy to say such a thing?"

The Chief Secretary of the Cabinet shared this with Director Oka of the Naval Office Naval Affairs Bureau and Oka replied: "The Navy is not in a position to formally say it doesn't desire war. All the Navy can say is that it has entrusted the matter to the Prime Minister."

That evening, President Suzuki of the Planning Board came to my private home with the following message from the War Minister: "Our further investigation has shown that the Navy doesn't want war. Then why doesn't the Navy Minister say so? If he says it plainly, I must consider it but, very regrettably, he has virtually entrusted the matter to the Prime Minister. If the Navy really is indecisive, the decision made at the September 6 Imperial Conference is fundamentally affected. In other words, this means that the Prime Minister, War, and Navy Ministers and the Chief of the Supreme Command who attended the Conference did not fully discharge their responsibility to assist the Emperor. Accordingly, we must resign en bloc, begin with a clean slate and formulate new plans all over again. There is no person apparent who would control the Army and Navy and work on a new plan. The only recourse to adoption is to induce a member of the Imperial Family to head the next Cabinet. The candidate most fit for this is Prince Higashikuni. I do not relish asking the Prime Minister to resign but, in light of the present situation, I hope the Throne will be petitioned to allow the appointment of Prince Higashikuni as the next Premier.

The next day, October 15, His Majesty received me in the audience and I reported: "Last night Tojo sent word that Prince Higashikuni should be chosen to head the next Cabinet."

His Majesty replied: "I thought Prince Higashikuni would become an ideal Chief of the General Staff but full caution must be exercised in regard to a member of the Imperial Family actually having a hand in politics. In peacetime it may be alright but, in view of the possibility of war, I consider it more improper for an Imperial Family member to come out. Its effect on the Imperial Family must be considered." Yet the Emperor was not totally opposed to Prince Higashikuni's appointment. On my way home, I met the Lord Keeper of the Privy Seal, Kido, and mentioned Prince Higashikuni's name. Kido did not seem interested in this project.

The same night, I paid a secret visit to Prince Higashikuni and informed him of the War Minister's views. When urged to rise to the occasion, His Highness replied: "The matter is too serious. Give me two or three days to think it over."

However, the prevailing situation was such that even a single day would not be wasted. I summoned all the Cabinet Ministers to the Japanese room of the official residence and, in individual talks with them, I stated the reasons for which the Cabinet had to resign en bloc. I gained their understanding, collected their resignation papers and proceeded to the Imperial Palace that evening.

War Minister Tojo Given Imperial Command

Thus, the Konoye Cabinet resigned en bloc. The following day, the senior statesmen held a conference, and the Imperial Command to organize the next Cabinet fell to War Minister Tojo. I think it was due to the proposal of the Lord Keeper of the Privy Seal, Kido, that War Minister Tojo was recommended to the Throne. But I do not think that by picking Tojo, Kido intended to invite war between Japan and the U.S. It appears to have been Kido's view that, since Tojo viewed beginning with a clean slate because of the Navy's lack of clarity, even if the Imperial Command fell to Tojo, he would not plunge into war at once. Kido's view seemed to be that, if the Imperial Command was Tojo's and the Emperor spoke about the matter, the War Minister would adopt a more cautious attitude.

The circumstances leading up to the change in the Cabinet were as stated above. On the surface, disunity was caused by conflicting views between the Prime Minister bent on continuing American-Japanese negotiations and the War Minister intending to disrupt them. As a result, the general resignation followed. Accordingly, the fall of the Imperial Command on the War Minister was calculated to be interpreted as abandonment of

American-Japanese negotiations and the opening of an American-Japanese War. But the fall of the Imperial Command on Tojo did not mean war at once because of the foregoing circumstances. Questions on this point were raised at the conference of senior statesmen who felt relieved when told by Kido that the fall of the Imperial Command would never signify immediate war between Japan and the U.S. After obtaining this assurance, they recommended the War Minister to the Throne for Premiership. This is what I heard later. I, therefore, sent a letter to Ambassador Grew after my resignation and told him that my resignation is not a result of the decision to begin a war between Japan and the U.S. but that there is still left substantial room for further American-Japanese negotiations.

Upon returning to Japan, Ambassador Nomura told me that the news of the Konoye Cabinet's resignation was received with shock in the United States. When the Cabinet was shifted to War Minister Tojo, the American government thought there was no longer any hope of American-Japanese negotiations materializing. Captain Turner, the officer whose ship carried the remains of the late Ambassador Saito to Japan and who maintained a friendship with Ambassador Nomura, called on him and said: "The Konoye Cabinet must have resigned because Premier Konoye abandoned hope for American-Japanese negotiations since the President would not respond favorably to his proposal for an interview with the President. However, the President did not reject the proposal outright. He merely wanted to make sure about two or three things beforehand. If the assurances were made, he would gladly see Premier Konoye. The procedure was initiated to send a personal message from the President to the Emperor reflecting this." A few days later, Captain Turner said "Objections were raised regarding sending a personal message to the Emperor because it would constitute interference in Japanese domestic politics. Hence, the idea was dropped."

Emperor Reserved Toward Supreme Commander

Recalling the difficult path of the American-Japanese negotiations, I am very impressed by the lack of unity between the Supreme Command and the Administration. The independence of military affairs from administrative matters had been troublesome for each succeeding cabinet. In the case of American-Japanese negotiations, while we were absorbed in the negotiations, the fighting services were fully engaged in preparations to cope with their rupture. What preparations were being made, I could not know. As a result, diplomacy could not keep pace with the military. They moved or mobilized ships and the U.S. awareness of this created suspicion about the sincerity of our diplomacy. In my view, the lack of unity between diplomacy and military affairs was the source of trouble.

At the time, heated arguments were made regarding whether or not Japan should fight the United States.

Prince Higashikuni was one of those advising cautions and once declared the Emperor alone would be able to save the situation. His Majesty told me, as well as Prince Higashikuni, that several times His Majesty was troubled by the military's action. His Highness Prince Higashikuni told His Majesty that it was inadvisable for His Majesty to remain in the role of a commentator. Prince Higashikuni is said to have told His Majesty that if he thought anything to be inadvisable, he should say so.

Thus, the Emperor was reserved and seldom expressed his own views. Prince Saionji and Count Makino had taught His Majesty not to take the initiative in adherence to the British-style constitution, but the Japanese constitution, fundamentally different from that of the British, exists on the premise of the Emperor's personal administration. Particularly regarding the matter of the Supreme Command, the government has no voice at all. It is the Emperor alone who can control both the government and the Supreme Command.

It is said that the Emperor should be passive in peacetime, but when the country stands at the crossroads of rising or falling, trouble is likely to occur. If the Emperor merely gives encouragement or advice as in England, military affairs and political diplomacy cannot advance in unison. This point was strongly felt in the course of the latest American-Japanese negotiations.

In conclusion, I should like to say one thing. Although His Majesty's attitude as the constitutional monarch was passive, his concern always was with the maintenance of peace in the Pacific. He tried to avoid plunging into an uncertain and great war and was seriously concerned about maintaining the heart of the 2,600-year-old national policy. It was very painful for me to witness His Majesty so deeply concerned over the matter.

THE END

Made in the USA
Las Vegas, NV
28 March 2023